Dorm Room Feng Shui

FIND YOUR GUA > FREE YOUR CHI ;-)

Katherine Olaksen

Elizabeth MacCrellish

Margaret M. Donahue

Storey Publishing

The mission of Storey Publishing is to serve our customers by publishing practical information that encourages personal independence in harmony with the environment.

Edited by Deb Burns, Siobhan Dunn and Sarah Guare
Cover design by Kent Lew
Text design by Wendy Palitz
Cover illustration by Kent Lew
Text production by Jennifer Jepson Smith
Indexed by Christine R. Lindemer, Boston Road Communications

Printed in the United States by Versa Press
10 9 8 7 6 5 4 3 2

Library of Congress Cataloging-in-Publication Data

Olaksen, Katherine.
    Dorm room feng shui : find your gua * free your chi / by Katherine Olaksen,
    Elizabeth MacCrellish & Margaret Donahue.
        p. cm.
    Includes bibliographical references and index.
    ISBN-13: 978-1-58017-592-0 (pbk. : alk. paper)
    1. Feng shui. 2. Dormitories—Miscellanea. I. MacCrellish, Elizabeth. II. Donahue,
    Margaret. III. Title.
BF1779.F4O43 2005
133.3'337—dc22

                                                    2005007469

Contents

Preface

This book is the result of a true collaboration. Elizabeth contributed her writing skills, Margaret contributed her in-depth knowledge of feng shui principles, and Katherine ensured that the focus of the book addressed the needs of college students everywhere.

As Katherine discovered when she sought to improve her dorm room using feng shui, it is difficult to find a helpful guide that provides solutions to the specific challenges facing people who live in small, shared spaces. Most books on the subject reference the living rooms, dining rooms, hallways, and other standard parts of houses and apartments. While this book is focused on the college dorm, much, if not all, of the advice given can be equally well applied to anyone living in cramped quarters, whether it be a studio apartment, boarding school dormitory, sailboat — you name it.

Bringing *Dorm Room Feng Shui* into being has been both challenging and fun for us. Our hope is that this book will help you to balance your chi, as well as help you to attract the people, energies, and events you most desire in your life. And, finally, we hope that the environment you create around you supports and clarifies your life's purpose.

Live your dreams!

Introduction

Oh no! Someone wants you to read *another* book? Excuse me, like you don't already have a stack of textbooks on your desk? (Okay, you sold them to throw a party for 300 of your closest friends, but same difference, right?)

Deep breath. Count to 10. Go to your happy place. There is no need to stress. This book is:

a. easier to read than Cliff Notes

b. going to make your life all dreamy like a Sunday morning eating Krispy Kreme donuts in bed while getting a foot massage (well, maybe not that exactly, but if you check out some of the suggestions in here, things are definitely going to improve — for sure).

However, let me be clear about one thing: Feng shui is as layered and complex as Egyptian hieroglyphics, and there are people who take feng shui very, very seriously. And I'm not trying to dis that, but what you need to understand is that this little book is not that. I'm all about **taking it lightly.** Which is not to say that we don't have a major problem to focus on here . . . Hello, have you seen the place where you're going to be spending many, many months of your life? Honestly, how does anyone expect to fit a computer, a printer, a refrigerator, a microwave, a stereo, a flatscreen TV, a desk, a bed, and a roommate, and all her stuff, into one small space? (Ha — just kidding about the flatscreen, of course.)

Well, outside of a sledgehammer and a couple of sticks of dynamite, there's not a whole heckuva lot you can do to change the size of your room. But what you can do is maximize the good energy and minimize the negative. How? Keep reading.

Take It or Leave It

Whether you're headed to school for the first time or returning for another year of shared, cramped quarters, you know several things. You want to be comfortable. You want to have some of your favorite things around. And, of course, you want your space to be fabulous.

What are you going to bring? Too much stuff, probably.

Decide carefully what to take to school, be selective, and choose deliberately. Keep in mind that everything is made up of vibrations and everything holds energy. All of your possessions contain energetic imprints of what was going on in your life when you acquired them and patterns of what has happened since then, so think carefully about what each one means.

Start out with as little as possible, along the way adding only things that you really love or that you really need. The nine oversized stuffed animals your boyfriend won for you at the fair might not really be a necessity.

Although it flies in the face of our consumer society, whose motto is Buy, Buy, Buy, the truth is that **less is more.** Nowhere is this truer than in a very small space. So when it comes to your room, step one is to focus on the clutter and clear it out — not like sending it on vacation, but for good. And in case you are wondering, clutter is anything that you don't use or anything that you don't love. Period. No exceptions. (Reread this paragraph until the concept sticks.)

The reason you want to ditch the clutter is that it holds you in place. Clutter prevents you from moving forward. If you feel you really can't let go of stuff, get a friend (or a condescending acquaintance) to help. The rule is love it, use it, or lose it.

Once you've hauled off those boxes and bags of clutter to a secondhand shop or the dump (and stopped at your favorite coffee shop for a double latte on the way back to celebrate your good work), you'll find a room with new space.

Don't rush to fill it back up. If you want new experiences to come into your life, you have to create the space for them. Also, do try to keep the area under your bed free and clear — it will help you get a good night's sleep.

Okay, now here's the one thing you didn't want to hear: The best thing you can do to liven up your room is to clean it. Not what you want to hear, but deal with it — it's the truth.

If it seems daunting, start small. Begin by opening the window and letting in some fresh air. Still there? You didn't collapse from the effort? Then you're ready for the big leagues.

Beg, borrow, or steal a vacuum and thoroughly vacuum the walls, the floor, your desk, your bed . . . everything.

Wash the surface area of your desk and bookshelves with some water and white vinegar. Or if you're feeling really Martha Stewart, spritz the air with some water and essence of orange for an energetic lift. Burn some incense, bring in fresh flowers, or get an inexpensive new plant. It sounds like a lot of work, but any one of these actions will lift the chi of your space, and doing more than one will really carbonate your soda.

Now, sure — who's got time to clean when there's so much partying to be done? True enough. But, space clearing doesn't have to be done every day. Do it when you feel stuck and are ready for something new.

Try space clearing before you begin to study for exams, before a big party, before a hot date, or before any other important activity. See what happens. You'll get hooked.

About Feng Shui

In the introduction, I said feng shui requires years of study to master . . . What? You didn't read the Introduction? Go on back there and read it, you slacker. Why do you think I'm writing this book? For my health? All right, stop whining. You're here now. Fine. I won't make you go back.

Here's the thing: Feng shui is an ancient and complex field of learning. In fact, there are several different methods of feng shui and each of them has its own layers upon layers of structure. It's a little intense (and boring). And besides, you've got too much studying to do already, so I'm gonna keep it short and sweet. Here are the Need to Knows.

There are three areas of feng shui that it would be helpful for you to know something about: chi (or ch'i), the elements, and yin and yang. (But if you're really getting into this and want to learn more, or have an overachieving complex, go to References and Recommended Reading at the back of this book where I list some terrific resources where you can get all the details.)

Chi is pronounced *chee* as in CHEEtos, CHEERios, or "oh my goodness, those jeans were so CHEAP." So what is it? Does it come in a jar, in a squeeze bottle? Can you buy the stuff? Don't think so. Chi is energy. It is inside you and all around you, so when you improve your chi, you improve your life.

Although it isn't molecular biology (which you probably dropped because you value your social life), improving your chi does take focus and intention. For example, if you're seconds away from crashing but have exams to study for, clear your desk. Yep. Take everything right off it. Wipe it down. Now, put back only those things that are **absolutely essential** (and no, your espresso machine is not an essential). If you've got stuff draped over the back of your chair, put it away. (DON'T chuck it all under the bed — c'mon now, you knew that one.)

For more ideas, check out the list to the right for simple ways to boost your chi and things to avoid that will reduce your chi to a small, crumbling, past-its-expiration-date Pop-Tart.

How to Bone Up Your Chi

✳ Turn off the lights and the loud music and get some deep, peaceful sleep.

✳ Eat like you understand that good food and lots of water will give you great skin and strong bones.

✳ Jump into a pool, play a little tennis, go for a bike ride, run, walk (some exercise . . . you know the drill).

✳ Meditate.

✳ Chill with your friends.

✳ Laugh and laugh.

✳ Read a book for pleasure.

✳ Sit and sleep with a solid wall at your back.

✳ Surround yourself with colors you love.

How to Kill Chi

✳ Start drinking coffee at 10 P.M. to get you through yet another all-nighter.

✳ Skip breakfast. Lunch on Twinkies. Dine on Doritos.

✳ Spend 12 hours in bed, 4 hours in a chair, and 8 hours on the sofa, daily.

✳ Take up smoking.

✳ Never leave your room. Fill your mind with fears and worry.

✳ Consume too much alcohol.

✳ OD on hyper-caffeinated beverages.

✳ Sleep or sit without a view of the door.

✳ Let clutter pile up around you.

The Elements (Sounds like an old disco band,

doesn't it? But I digress . . .)

Does your life sometimes feel as if you're standing barefoot on a beach ball with waves coming in and pulling the sand out from under the ball and it's all you can do to keep upright? If that sounds vaguely familiar, then you will relate to this concept. **It's all about balance.** Or as the French say, bah-LAHNce.

Five elements are at the heart of feng shui (wood, fire, earth, metal, water) and the goal is to achieve a balance among them.

Below is a summary of the particular attributes for each of the five elements. As you look around your room, see how each of these elements is represented. Now, are they in balance or, for example, do you have too much water? Maybe you've been

Element	Attribute
Wood	Blue and green, columns, stripes, spring, trees, plants, flowers
Fire	Red, triangles, summer, sunlight, lamps, candles, people, animals
Earth	Yellow and brown, squares, late summer, pottery, adobe, clay, brick
Metal	White and gray, circles, ovals, autumn, gold, silver, aluminum, brass
Water	Black, free and flowing forms, winter, glass, mirrors, windows

Element	Generates	Destroys	Reduces
Wood	fire	earth	water
Water	wood	fire	metal
Metal	water	wood	earth
Earth	metal	water	fire
Fire	earth	metal	wood

feeling like you're on an emotional roller coaster and would like things to calm down. Bring in some wood to "sponge up" the excess water energy and watch what happens.

Review the chart above. Notice how all of the different elements interact.

Take a look around your room. Do you have too much of one or another element? You may need to bring in an opposing element to bring about balance.

If you have too much:

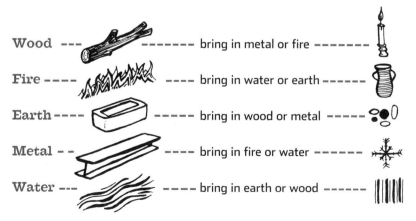

Wood --- ------- bring in metal or fire -------

Fire ---- ---- bring in water or earth ------

Earth ---- ---- bring in wood or metal -----

Metal -- ---- bring in fire or water ------

Water --- ---- bring in earth or wood ------

Yin and Yang

Because I'm talking about balance, I've got to dish on yin and yang. When things are out of whack, it's likely you've got too much yin or too much yang. How will you know which? Easy.

First of all, everything is composed of yin and yang. You can't have one without the other. Together they bring balance and form the whole. But here's the important thing: Yin and yang are always measured in relation to each other.

Next to yang, yin can be small, dark, heavy, and sad. Winter is a yin season and midnight is the most yin time of night.

Next to yin, yang can be big, bright, light, and joyful. Summer is a yang season and noon is the most yang time of day.

Yeah, now you're saying, "Who wants sad and heavy energy? Let's just have all yang!" Uh, no. Didn't you ever see the movie *Pleasantville?* For those who might have missed it, Reese Witherspoon and Tobey Maguire go back to the 1950s when everything is happy all the time. Gak. The point is, shadows *and* light, people. That's what we're going for. Not all shadows. Not all light. **The goal is to achieve balance.** However, balance does not mean equal. Typically, a balanced environment will be about 60 percent yang and 40 percent yin. More yang than yin, but not too much more.

Look around and see how the principles of yin and yang operate in your daily life. You know how there's that friend who can always make you laugh even when things aren't going well? And of course we all know that friend who can't seem to focus on anything but the negative (think Eeyore). If you're spending all your days with Eeyore, don't be surprised if you start feeling down.

The same applies to your studies. Be sure to take a fun, easy, or interesting class each semester to balance out all the hardcore requirements. And, at the risk of sounding like a parent, try putting some vegetables on your plate and avoid eating a bag of chips for breakfast. Too much junk food will do more than clog your arteries. It will clog your chi and make you feel sluggish, which in turn upsets your yin/yang balance.

Here are some attributes of yin and yang to help you become more attuned to the influences around you.

Personality Qualities

Yin	Yang
Feminine	Masculine
Quiet	Loud
Spiritual	Materialistic
Emotional	Physical
Negative	Positive
Sad	Happy
Introverted	Extroverted
Calm	Excited
Soft-spoken	Outspoken
Reserved	Bold

Spatial Qualities

Yin	Yang
Soft	Hard
Dark	Light
Cold	Hot
Curved	Straight
Low	High
Small	Large
Rounded	Angular
Back	Front
Wide	Narrow
Floral	Geometric

So, how can you balance yourself, balance your roommate, balance your room, balance even your schedule? Bring in the opposite quality. (**Note: Do not go overboard.** You do not want to go from one extreme to the other. Practice moderation.)

For example, let's imagine you have a very quiet roommate who never goes out. You would like it if your roommate got more socially involved. What would be the best path forward? Should you invite your roommate to join you and a couple of friends to see a movie? Should you bring your shy roommate to an outdoor rock concert and introduce her to the joys of mosh-pit dancing? It's up to you, really.

Everything operates in relation to its surroundings. What is right for one situation may not be appropriate at another time. You have to consider everything in the context of its environment. **Strive for what feels good**, what feels best. Your intuition is your best guide.

A key factor to understand is that there is no right and wrong. Yin and yang are two complementary yet opposite forces. Each exists in relation to the other. They represent the duality of the universe. When you change something, you are simply altering the balance of the yin and yang qualities.

Bagua in Brief

Ba. As in bah humbug. **Gua.** Say it now, GWAH. That's it —
BahGwah. If you're going to do some feng shui fixes to your
room, you've got to understand at least a little something about
the *bagua*. One way to think about it is that *ba* means eight and
gua means section. Essentially, the bagua is a way to divide any
space into eight separate pieces that are held together by a
ninth — the center.

In the following pages, I will explain how to identify each
gua with a small grid that highlights the section you are reading about. For example, if you want to improve money issues,
you should focus on the fourth gua, which represents prosperity. But first you need to understand how your room sits
within the bagua.

Take a piece of paper and sketch out the shape of your room with the door at the bottom of your page (Figure 1). Be sure to outline the furniture. Then, draw a box around the drawing of your room and make a tic-tac-toe grid within the box you just drew. You should have nine squares in the grid (Figure 2).

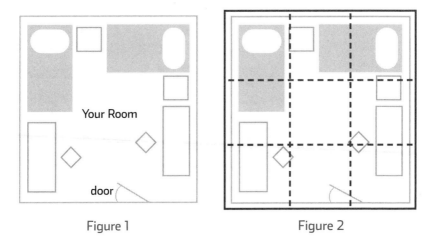

Figure 1   Figure 2

Now put numbers and words into each of the nine squares, like this (Figure 3). Take your bagua and line it up so that the row of boxes with Knowledge (**8**), Career (**1**), and Helpful People (**6**) are on the same line as the entry door to your room. It's very possible your room is not a perfect square, but not to worry. If there is a part of your room that extends beyond the box of the bagua, that can be a good thing — like an extra pinch of sugar in your coffee or a dollop of whipped cream on a dish of ice cream. If, on the other hand, there is a section of your room that doesn't quite fill out the bagua, that can mean this is

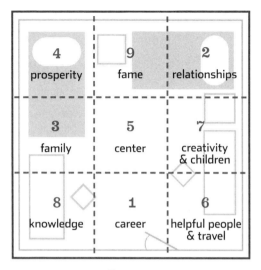

4 prosperity	9 fame	2 relationships
3 family	5 center	7 creativity & children
8 knowledge	1 career	6 helpful people & travel

Figure 3

an area that needs a bit of extra help. Either way, let the improvements begin!

Over the next several pages, each gua is laid out for you in detail. The 3-Minute Questionnaire (page 18) will help you identify which areas of your life need some balance and improvement. Feel free to head there now, or stick with me another moment here as I give you an example of how this information can be used and applied. This is your program, baby. You know what works best for you. I'm just here to provide suggestions and guidance. (**Note:** If you skip ahead, remember that the point is to bring **your own personal flair** to the gua using my guidelines as a jumping-off point. There are no cookie-cutter solutions. It is how you set your intention that brings power to these actions.)

Imagine there are two roommates named Alex and Allie. On Alex's questionnaire, her eighth gua received three checks. Alex looks at the front left corner of her room and rolls her eyes. This is the area of Knowledge. Oh boy, thinks Alex. Not only is her laundry basket filled with weeks of wash she keeps meaning to do, but on top of the laundry is also a knitting bag replete with needles and yarn and a partially finished scarf that Alex began back when everybody was into knitting. Next to the laundry basket are some posters Alex and Allie were going to put up but never did. The floor is bare and there is no room on the shelves for books because Alex has her stereo set up there.

Hmmm, no wonder Alex is having academic trouble. This area is filled with clutter, unfinished projects, and electronic equipment — all of which **block the chi** in this gua. How can she expect to think clearly when there's all this *stuff* in the way?

But what about Allie, you might be wondering. She is doing great in all of her classes. Why aren't her academics suffering? Well, Allie has done a little feng shui cure to counter Alex's mess. First, Allie cleaned her desk and cleared off all of the clutter. Then she placed a square yellow cloth under her computer and arranged her books neatly. Allie hung above the desk the framed certificate she got from winning an 8th grade spelling bee. And oh, yeah — she studies a lot. Heh. You actually don't think it's *all* magic do you? Now, come on. Feng shui will help to improve the energy flow. It will be easier to get to class on time and to study if you don't have heavy blocks in your Knowledge gua, but feng shui doesn't replace studying. Did you really think it would?

9 Gua Fixes (for under 99¢)

Feng shui changes and enhancements can be cheap and creative. Here are nine ideas, one for each gua, to get you going.

Gua	Fix
1	Tear a piece of cardboard into a free-form shape (no sharp edges). Cover it in aluminum foil. Pile spare change on it.
2	Take an envelope. Color it red. Seal it. Make a small slit. Tuck in notes about things for which you want forgiveness.
3	Grow a small plant or flowers from seed.
4	Cover a soda can in purple (tissue, paper, or paint) and use it as a bank.
5	Repeat this daily: "I am well balanced and grounded."
6	Draw a picture of your dad and list his best qualities.
7	Write down the names of seven people you think are creative. Then list the creative qualities you share with each of them.
8	Sculpt your hand out of clay, Play-Doh, or papier-mâché and keep it in this area to represent the hand of wisdom.
9	In red ink, write an affirmation stating how you intend to be known (in the present tense) and place it in this area.

3-Minute Questionnaire

Here's an easy way to identify the areas of your life that could use the most help. Answer each question below with a yes or no, but don't overthink it. Go with your gut response and move on.

1. Do you know exactly what you are going to do when you graduate? ☐ Yes ☐ No

2. Do you often feel anxious? ☐ Yes ☐ No

3. When you get sick, do you tend to have problems with your ears or kidneys? ☐ Yes ☐ No

4. Do you have a great relationship with your mom? ☐ Yes ☐ No

5. Are you able to attract and maintain a romantic relationship? ☐ Yes ☐ No

6. Do you hold grudges? ☐ Yes ☐ No

7. Do you hold on to anger? ☐ Yes ☐ No

8. Do you love family and holiday get-togethers? ☐ Yes ☐ No

9. Do you lack the energy to start new projects? ☐ Yes ☐ No

10. Do you feel that life just works for you? ☐ Yes ☐ No

11. Are you often broke? ☐ Yes ☐ No

12. Do you often volunteer or give your time to others? ☐ Yes ☐ No

13. Do you often have stomach problems? ☐ Yes ☐ No

14. Do you feel in control of your life? ☐ Yes ☐ No

15. Are you a creature of habit? ☐ Yes ☐ No

16. Do you have a great relationship with your dad? ☐ Yes ☐ No

17. Do you often get headaches? ☐ Yes ☐ No

18. When you ask for help, do you usually get it? ☐ Yes ☐ No

19. Do you feel comfortable speaking your truth? ☐ Yes ☐ No

20. Do you take life too seriously?	☐ Yes	☐ No
21. Do you laugh often?	☐ Yes	☐ No
22. Do you have trouble making decisions?	☐ Yes	☐ No
23. Is getting good grades important to you?	☐ Yes	☐ No
24. Do you feel you can never get enough time alone?	☐ Yes	☐ No
25. Are really passionate about something?	☐ Yes	☐ No
26. Do you feel good when people recognize you?	☐ Yes	☐ No
27. Do you like the image you project?	☐ Yes	☐ No

NOW, place a check mark next to any answer below that corresponds with yours. Any gua that has two or three checks next to it represents an area that could use some improvement. Flip to the corresponding page indicated to read up on ways to improve this.

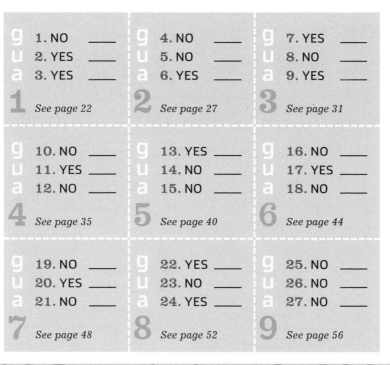

g u a 1
1. NO ____
2. YES ____
3. YES ____
See page 22

g u a 2
4. NO ____
5. NO ____
6. YES ____
See page 27

g u a 3
7. YES ____
8. NO ____
9. YES ____
See page 31

g u a 4
10. NO ____
11. YES ____
12. NO ____
See page 35

g u a 5
13. YES ____
14. NO ____
15. NO ____
See page 40

g u a 6
16. NO ____
17. YES ____
18. NO ____
See page 44

g u a 7
19. NO ____
20. YES ____
21. NO ____
See page 48

g u a 8
22. YES ____
23. NO ____
24. YES ____
See page 52

g u a 9
25. NO ____
26. NO ____
27. NO ____
See page 56

Consolidated Bagua Chart

Prosperity 4

I Ching Trigram*: Wind
Element: Wood
Color: Purple
Shape: Columns, rectangles
Body Part: Hips
Enhancements: Water, plants, valuables, jewelry, piggy bank, jade plant, fan, mobile

Family 3

I Ching Trigram*: Thunder
Element: Wood
Color: Green
Shape: Columns, rectangles
Body Parts: Feet, liver
Enhancements: Family photos, trees, plants, blue and green stripes

Knowledge 8

I Ching Trigram*: Mountain
Element: Earth
Color: Blue
Shape: Squares
Body Parts: Hands, back
Enhancements: Diplomas, academic certificates, books

*Trigrams relate to the yin yang energetic quality of each gua. See the I Ching resources at the end of the book to learn more.

Fame & Reputation 9

I Ching Trigram*: Fire
Element: Fire
Color: Red
Shape: Triangles
Body Parts: Eyes, heart
Enhancements: Sun, people, animals, lights, red flowers

Relationships 2

I Ching Trigram*: Earth
Element: Earth
Color: Pink
Shape: Squares
Body Parts: Stomach, spleen
Enhancements: Picture of a couple, pair of items, seashells, pottery, clay, photo of mom

Center 5

I Ching Trigram*: None
Element: Earth
Color: Yellow
Shape: Squares
Body Part: Stomach
Enhancements: Urns, terra-cotta, clay pots, square rugs

Children & Creativity 7

I Ching Trigram*: Lake
Element: Metal
Color: White
Shape: Ovals, circles, arches
Body Parts: Mouth, lungs
Enhancements: Playful objects, toys, friends, rocks, bath salts

Career 1

I Ching Trigram*: Water
Element: Water
Color: Black
Shape: Free-flowing shapes
Body Parts: Ears, kidneys
Enhancements: Mirrors, ideal career image, roads, paths

Helpful People & Travel 6

I Ching Trigram*: Heaven
Element: Metal
Color: Gray
Shape: Ovals, circles, arches
Body Part: Head
Enhancements: Angels, metal wind chimes, photos of mentors

4	9	2
3	5	7
8	**1**	6

"Most success springs from an obstacle or failure. I became a cartoonist largely because I failed in my goal of becoming a successful executive."

SCOTT ADAMS, creator of Dilbert

GUA **1** Career

If you have a number of check marks here, your Career gua could use some attention. I'm not going to ask what you want to be when you grow up. This gua is about more than just a job. It's really about your life path, your future. Hmm, does the word *future* make you want to pull the covers over your head? Is deciding what you're going to wear tonight as far ahead as you can look? Of course it is. I know you could use a little help, and that's what I'm here for!

If you stress about your future, you can't be that happy with your current goals, or maybe you don't know where you're headed. If what you're doing doesn't excite you, generate your curiosity, or make you feel connected to your best self, reflect on why you're doing it. Are you doing it because you want to? Or are you doing it because you think it is what someone else expects of you? You'll be happiest when you **choose what you really want** to do and put a plan in place to get there. If your activities are uninspiring, make a plan to replace them with something that blows your skirt up!

If you don't know what your passions are, don't freak out; lots of people don't know. Here are some things to do that will help improve the chi in your Career gua, and all good things will follow.

Solutions to Gua 1

1 Bring the **water element** into this section of the room. It could be a photo of a waterfall, the ocean, or a lake, or a fountain. Set up an aquarium. Drape some wavy, fluid fabric — anything soft and flowing, such as velvet or chenille.

2 Introduce the **color black** or midnight blue here. White will also strengthen this area.

3 Think **winter.** Make paper snowflakes or find a little snowman figurine. Clip a photo of some hot snowboarders from a magazine. Remember, it's all about *you*. What makes you think of winter in a positive way?

4 A very simple solution is to place a glass of water in this gua. Just be sure to freshen it daily for good chi flow.

5 Another element of the first gua is its connection to midnight and your inner self. **Echo midnight** here with a moon and stars, or something inky black, or pin up a poem about midnight. You'll come up with something cool, for sure.

6 Putting a **mirror** in this gua is a good idea as long as it does not face the bed.

7 Bring in **circles,** ovals, and arch shapes. Put a round rug here, or use an oval picture frame. This will bring in the metal element, which strengthens water. An oval-shaped, metal-framed mirror would be ideal!

8 **Clear clutter.** Repair anything broken. Keep windows and mirrors clean. Remove all dust and cobwebs.

9 Another thing you might do with this space is place an object that represents what you would like to do with your life. For example, you want to be president someday: Bring a stuffed donkey or elephant (depending on your party affiliation) into this gua. You want to travel the world: Put on display that souvenir Eiffel Tower your aunt brought you back. You get the idea.

As far as health is concerned, this gua is associated with the ears, kidneys, bladder, bodily fluids, and the reproductive system. Sometimes an uneasiness with your career choice or lack of clarity about your path in life emerges as a health imbalance in one of these areas. And remember, opportunities often emerge at the most unexpected times. Be open to possibility.

gua 1

What can be in	What should be out
Water, water images	Candles
Black, midnight blue, white	Reds, greens
Free-flowing shapes, ovals, arches, circles	Triangular shapes, pointy things
Metal-framed mirrors, pictures of your ideal career	Too many plants and electronics
Images of paths or roads	Clutter, obstacles, anything broken or in disrepair

Feng Shui for Hire

Here are some ideas to use feng shui to help you find the perfect summer job or land the internship you've been dreaming about.

🌀 **Write an affirmation** about the perfect summer position and place it in the center of your desk (you can put it under your computer or even in a drawer). Or put the affirmation in the Career gua of your room. The affirmation could go something like this: "I am so grateful to have the perfect summer job doing . . . [insert job here] . . ."

🌀 **Make a "creation box."** Every time you have an idea or inspiration about what you would like to do over the summer, cut out a picture or words that describe the situation. You can also write the words or draw the picture yourself. Place the images into the box. Visualize your dream coming true.

🌀 **Give thanks in advance** for receiving the perfect internship coming to you effortlessly and easily. Daily, write statements of gratitude in a small journal or notebook.

🌀 **Hang a small crystal ball** or wind chime in the Career gua. As you place it, think about how it will feel to receive the job or internship you seek.

🌀 Most important of all, **believe that you will get the right job** or position for yourself. Spend more time believing in yourself. Feed a positive stream of thought and dismiss all fear, worry, and anxiety.

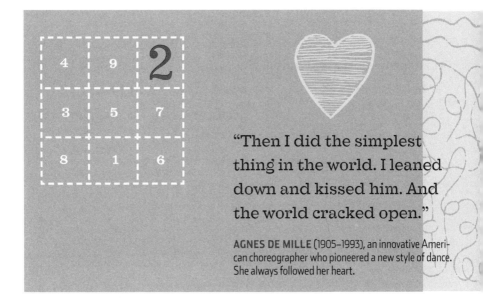

4	9	2
3	5	7
8	1	6

"Then I did the simplest thing in the world. I leaned down and kissed him. And the world cracked open."

AGNES DE MILLE (1905–1993), an innovative American choreographer who pioneered a new style of dance. She always followed her heart.

GUA 2 Relationships

If you landed here, your Relationships gua needs some attention. Hmmm . . . wild guess: You're looking to hook up with somebody special. Or you've got someone on the line but need some help reeling in that hottie. You're in luck. A little work on the back right corner of your room, and watch your romantic life heat up.

Of course, not all relationships are hookups — duh. A primary relationship associated with this gua is your mom. We're also talking about improving things with your roommate; staying on good terms with your professors; and having good, caring friends.

When you want to attract a new relationship or strengthen an existing one, this is the area of your room that you want to improve. First things first. How kind and loving are you to yourself? Do you tend to be very hard on yourself? I sure hope not. But if you are like a lot of people, you may be your own worst critic. Try to lighten up. Certainly the idea is to lighten up the energy in this gua. **Pink is the ruling color.** Think sunsets, mid-afternoon, end of summer, warmth, heat, romance. Yeah, baby!

Another key to improving your relationships is to avoid putting single items in this area. Also avoid images of people or animals walking apart or with their backs to each other. Instead, put a pair of something in this corner. **Think in twos.**

This is the place you want to put pottery (lucky you if this corner of the room is brick!), natural crystals, and anything earthy, especially if it has yellow or pink tones. To really pump up the volume, incorporate the color red or some candles (especially yellow candles — don't worry if you aren't allowed to burn them; it's enough simply to have them there), hang a lantern, or bring in some lights.

I want you to be good with your friends, tight with your roommate, cool with your mom, and connected to a total babe. Here are some things to do that will smooth the lumps out of your relationships.

Solutions to Gua 2

1 Think unconditional love and forgiveness. Release all angst. (Yeah, right, you say.) Okay, okay. Try this: Write down your wish for true love and a gentle heart on a piece of pink paper. Be sure to **write in the present tense,** as if it is happening now. Not in the future. Tuck the paper into this area with a clear intention.

2 Display a **happy picture** of you with your mom here.

3 Include squares and triangles. A great thing for this spot is a geometric puzzle.

4 Place something **earthy** in this corner, such as a beautiful clay or earthenware pot.

5 Use pinks, reds, and yellows in this area.

6 Be sure to put **a pair of something** in this gua: two candles, two elephants, two loons, an image of a loving couple. Get creative! What makes you think of love and kindness? Whatever it is, be sure to put in two.

7 Light a **candle** (especially a red one) with the intention of attracting or strengthening a relationship. (Just be sure to extinguish it before you leave the room!)

8 This gua is earth, so don't put your fountain here — earth and water make mud!

9 No black! No pictures of you sitting on a rock by yourself! Do you have a great picture of you and your friends? This is where you want to put it.

As far as health is concerned, this gua is associated with your stomach, spleen, immune system, and digestion. Problems with relationships, holding grudges or not being forgiving, and unresolved issues with your mother can manifest as health imbalances in these areas.

gua 2

What can be in	What should be out
Clay pots, terra-cotta pots	Single items, images of single items
Pink, red, yellow	White, gray
Squares, triangles	Circles, ovals, arches
A pair of something	Water, water images, fountains
Candles, lights, computers, microwave, TV, stereos	Anything metallic, such as photo frames or sculptures
Red flowers, seashells	All clutter, any obstacles, anything broken or in disrepair

4	9	2
3	5	7
8	1	6

"Human beings are the only creatures on earth that allow their children to come back home."

BILL COSBY, comic genius, actor, and writer

GUA 3 Family

How are things with the folks? Hmm. Was that a shrug? Let's be clear. If you have a lot of check marks here, there's some disruptive energy in your Family gua that needs to be taken care of. Or perhaps you are flirting with launching a project and need a boost. Either way, you're in the right place. The third gua is all about your family and ancestors. But oddly enough, it is also about beginnings.

If family concerns seem to be occupying your mind lately, this is the area you want to focus on. Are you missing your grandparents? Are they ill? Have you had a fight with one of your parents, or both of them? Maybe someone in your tribe is facing a serious struggle and you want to send him or her good energy. If you have pictures or mementos that represent your family, this is the best spot to place them. By the way, don't limit yourself to thinking that this has to be about just blood relatives. If you think of someone as family, this is where you want to keep his or her presence in your room.

Now, all of us go through ups and downs with our families. We love 'em, we hate 'em. We can't wait to get home for the holidays. We never want to see them again. It's the nature of the beast. But whatever your relationship with your family, you need to get very clear about it in order to create balance in your own life.

Are you trying to break away from an old path and start something new? Well, then, you're in luck. New paths are cut and forged here. This gua is associated with spring. Think ground breaking, buds, and a **fresh start.** Clear and energize this area and you will find your new endeavors taking flight.

Solutions to Gua 3

1 Bring in the **green**. Bright, spring, healthy green. It could be a green plant; if so, be sure to keep it healthy. (If you have a plant here and it is dried up and dying, you know what to do.)

2 Set three stems of bamboo in a small vase or glass of water.

3 Display **pictures of your parents**, grandparents, people you consider family.

4 If you have an image or a wooden sculpture of a tree, this is the place to put it.

5 Write an affirmation expressing your desire for, or appreciation of, strong **family ties**.

6 Pictures or representational art of a foot or feet would be great here.

7 Thunder is a major element of this gua. Think of a way to introduce the **energy of thunder**, even if it's just putting up the word *thunder* in big strong letters. Got some bongo drums? Put them here.

8 If you're lucky enough to have an east-facing window in this gua, count your blessings. If not, try to capture the spirit of **early morning**. If you have a book about songbirds or, better yet, a songbird figurine, that would power up this area.

9 If you have a wall here, paint it with blue and green **stripes**. If you're not allowed to paint, hang some blue-and-green-striped fabric.

As far as health is concerned, if you are having feet or liver problems, doing some good work in this area will definitely help. Think of your feet as the roots to your family. Unresolved issues with your parents, grandparents, siblings, or other family members can emerge as health problems here. The Family gua is also affiliated with the gallbladder and big bones. If you want to strengthen your overall health, this is the area that you need to work on.

gua 3

What can be **in**	What should be **out**
Green	Red, black
Wood	Metal
Water	Fire
Plants, seedlings	Dark, heavy items that don't promote growth
Family pictures, mementos	Candles

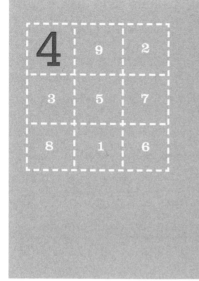

"Be content with what you have, rejoice in the way things are. When you realize there is nothing lacking, the whole world belongs to you."

LAO TZU (570–490 BCE), Chinese philosopher and a contemporary of Confucius

GUA 4! Prosperity

How's the old bank account? Feeling strapped? Do you often find yourself worrying about money? If you answered yes to these questions, you've landed in the right place to improve your financial situation. The fourth gua is all about wealth, abundance, and the feeling of prosperity. Great, you say as you play solitaire with your maxed-out credit cards.

Okay, that's enough sarcasm out of you. Here's the thing: The first step in building abundance around you is to shake off a sense of poverty or lack. You know the old phrase "You have to have money to make money?" Well, this is kind of the same thing. You have to feel and see your blessings right now in order for them to grow and multiply. When we recognize the blessings in our life, we become open and receptive to wealth and abundance. The worst thing you can do is focus on what you don't have. Doing that will only reinforce your feelings of being without or deprived. Everything will feel pinched and tight.

So how to increase the sensation of abundance and prosperity? Start giving out **what you want to receive**. Generosity and philanthropy are important aspects of prosperity. The more you give, the more you get back in return. I'm not talking about donating a new library to your campus (as if you could!). Give of your time, your energy, your compassion — these are all riches to be shared. Listening to a friend who is having problems, serving up meals at a soup kitchen, holding open the door for a person with packages (I'd like to think you would always do that, but whatever) — these are all ways of **putting out good energy** to the world, and it will come back to you. You name it, the opportunity to give to the world is there. As you give, give from your heart.

Another solution is to increase your use of purple: deep, rich purple. It is no surprise that purple is associated with royalty and prestige in many cultures. Two other colors that can help here are black and green, both of which support and strengthen this gua. (Black symbolizes water, and green represents wood.)

Wind is associated with this gua, and increasing its presence in this area of your room is important. Think of your ship coming in on a steady yet gentle breeze. Remember not to ask for too much force; you don't want gusting winds. By the same token, you don't want still, stagnant air either. A light, steady breeze that carries in new opportunities and new connections and carries you to new ground is what you are looking for.

Increase Prosperity Without Spending a Dime

Being philanthropic is a great way to enhance your own prosperity and attract synchronicity. Don't think you have to give money. You can donate skills, knowledge, or time. Remember, what you put out into the world comes back to you. When you give freely of yourself, you will get even more in return.

- **Volunteer** to tutor less-fortunate children.
- **Spend a few hours each week** working in a soup kitchen.
- **Spend a Saturday a month** helping out in an animal shelter.
- **Donate an afternoon** to a local community organization such as Girl Scouts or a YMCA program.
- **Visit a nearby nursing home** and offer to read the paper or a book to an elderly person who has trouble seeing.
- Remember to choose **an activity you love** or an organization you respect.

If you are feeling low or wish you had someone helping you, get out and give of yourself. Helping others helps take your mind off your own concerns, and you may just make an important connection that carries you farther along on your path.

So are you ready to pump up the volume on your sense of wealth and abundance? Let's do it.

Solutions to Gua 4

1 It's always important to **clear away clutter** and anything broken, but here most of all. Don't project an image of poverty or lack in your area of prosperity.

2 Bring in a **jade plant.** Jade is the money plant, so be sure to keep it healthy. (A word to the wise: Jade plants don't like too much water.)

3 Got a **piggy bank?** Put it here, baby.

4 Another trick is to place a piggy bank under your bed but still visible and within reach.

5 Want a really simple, really inexpensive thing to do? Write down what you have right now in your life that you are grateful for. Focus on everything you already have. Make an **affirmation** of gratitude for all your wealth. Tuck this piece of paper in this area. (See, didn't cost a dime!)

6 Bring in the **royal colors,** lots of purple and gold.

7 What do you associate with wealth? A poster of Donald Trump? A magazine cover with women in gorgeous dresses and diamonds? Put 'em up here.

8 Another key (no-cost) activity that will help you improve this area of your life is to **keep a journal** in which you write down three things each day that you are grateful for. As your list grows, so too will your abundance.

9 Get a glass jar and dump your spare change into it.

As far as health is concerned, the Prosperity gua is associated with the hips and pelvic area. It is also connected to your respiratory system. Worries about not having enough money can manifest as hip, leg, or breathing problems. Try to focus on feeling secure and knowing that you have more than enough.

gua 4

What can be **in**	What should be **out**
Purple, green, black, gold	White, yellow, pastels
Wood, water	Fire, earth
Coins, jewels	Candles
Most precious valuables	Cheapest, least valued items
Fountains	Clay pots, terra-cotta
Wind chimes, mobiles	Too many metal items

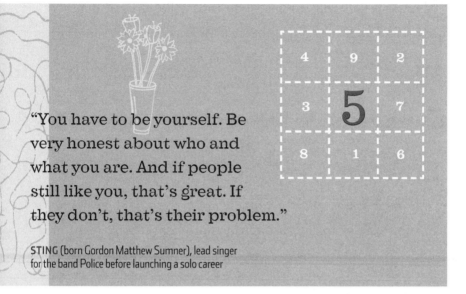

"You have to be yourself. Be very honest about who and what you are. And if people still like you, that's great. If they don't, that's their problem."

STING (born Gordon Matthew Sumner), lead singer for the band Police before launching a solo career

GUA 5 The Center

How well do you know yourself? How often do you ignore your gut instincts and follow someone else's idea or plan of action? If you need to get clearer about who you truly are and what is best for you, this is the place to start.

The Center gua is all about you. Are you tired? Burnt out? Do you feel scattered and never able to do the things you really want to do? Do you even know what it is you want? If you answered yes to any of these questions, let's make some changes to this area so that what's most important to you and your life begins to regain center stage.

The element of this gua is earth, which is all about security, stability, and groundedness. Earth energy is practical and resilient. To strengthen this area, bring in lots of yellow. Browns and tans are also good, because they reinforce the earth element.

This is the gua that rules the stomach, so if an overload of stress or anxiety has been causing you to have tummy troubles, examine what you have in this area of your room and clear out those elements that do not support the earth element. For instance, water turns earth into mud, so this is not the place for a fountain or a blue rug. What you want here are square shapes and patterns in natural earth tones.

Solutions to Gua 5

 Create **open space.**

 Hang a crystal from the center of this area to help you stay grounded.

 Place a square rug in the middle of your room.

 Meditate to gain serenity and clarity.

5 Add yellow, such as a vase of fresh yellow flowers.

6 Wear brown to increase the energy of stability and security.

7 Get some exercise or **treat yourself to a massage.** Do this with the intention of improving your sense of calm.

8 Play some **soothing music**. Chants are particularly well suited to improve the balance in this area.

9 Working in clay is a great activity to increase centeredness. If you can, get some clay and make a square tile. When things in your life start to get overwhelming, bring out the tile and use it as a reminder to **keep things simple** and bring yourself down to earth.

As far as health is concerned, the Center gua is about your overall well-being. If you abuse your body by not eating the right foods or not getting enough quality sleep, you will likely have a general feeling of unwellness. This is exacerbated by anxiety and worry. Pay attention to how you care for yourself. Good health is central to a good life.

gua 5

What can be in	What should be out
Urns, terra-cotta, clay pots	Water
Brown, yellow, orange	Blue, gray, purple
Squares	Circles and ovals
Yoga	Break dancing
Tai chi	Mirrors

Change at Your Center

If you have some bad habits or addictive behaviors you would like to change, here are some ideas that could help. Remember, one of the keys to changing behavior is to put more focus on where you are headed and less time and energy on the current situation. You attract to yourself whatever thoughts and feelings you feed, so feed the good ones!

🌀 **Remove everything** from your environment that reflects or reinforces the behavior you are trying to change . . . pictures, posters, books, clothes, knickknacks, you name it. Your environment is a reflection of yourself. Surround yourself with things that represent the way you intend to be, not necessarily the way you are right now.

🌀 **Hang a poster or picture** on your wall or inside your closet door that represents your new self or the person you intend to become.

🌀 **Meditate for 15 to 20 minutes daily.** Visualize the changes. Ask for strength and guidance.

🌀 In the present tense, **write down one or two sentences** about the behavior or habit that you wish to cultivate. (Note: It's the opposite of what you want to give up or quit.) Every morning after you get out of bed, sit quietly, look toward the ceiling, and read to yourself or recite aloud the statement describing your new behavior. Repeat for at least 17 seconds of uninterrupted thought. Focus on what you are bringing in, not what you are letting go of. For example: To reduce food cravings, try saying, "I choose foods that keep my body lean, fit, and at an ideal weight. I choose foods that increase my health and energize me."

4	9	2
3	5	7
8	1	**6**

> "I feel that there is an angel inside me whom I am constantly shocking."

JEAN COCTEAU (1889–1963), French writer, visual artist, and groundbreaking avant-garde filmmaker

GUA 6 Helpful People & Travel

Are you feeling like nothing ever goes right? Are you starting to wonder whether the gods are against you? Maybe it always seems the class you want most is full by the time you get to register or you keep missing the opportunity to hook up with the crush you've been secretly lusting after. If so, you're focused on the right place. The Helpful People and Travel gua is about **synchronicity** and once you straighten out the energies here, you will start to feel that one good event just leads to another in a perfect way. The help you need will manifest as if by magic.

This is the area of your inner guide and guardian angels. Create a place to honor them and make their spirits feel welcome. For example, find a piece of soft gray cloth such as velvet or chenille — think of gray as the color of turtle doves. Place the cloth on a clean surface and set some objects there that you associate with the spiritual or sacred. Metal is the element for this gua, so choose things made from gold, silver, brass, or aluminum. You could also gather up stones — especially smooth white or gray stones. Round or oval pieces of marble are ideal.

When you need help, write your request on a piece of paper and tuck it into this special place with a clear intention. Don't hesitate to ask your helpers for what you want. That's what they're here for!

If people are making comments about you that you're sarcastic, nosy, or downright mean sometimes, try to bring some balance to this gua. If your nature is a bit too sharp and critical, it's likely this metal area is out of whack. On the other hand, if you have too little metal, you might feel like you never say what you mean and communication is difficult for you. You may feel scattered and confused. Again, focus on creating balance in this gua and you will begin to communicate clearly what it is you want and how you want things to be.

Another thing to keep in mind is that this gua is associated with your dad, so if things aren't entirely rosy on the relationship front with your father, try one of the fixes below to boost the energy, and see whether things start feeling better.

Solutions to Gua 6

1 Place an **angel,** guardian creature, or fairy here.

2 Add a great picture of your dad.

3 Hang a six-rod metal wind chime.

4 Put up pictures of **places you want to visit.**

5 Start noticing serendipity in the world around you and put small tokens of thanks here for it.

6 Do you have a **mentor** or someone else who has been a big help to you in the past? Put her picture here or something that reminds you of her and her care for you.

7 If there is a teacher, professor, or leader in your field whom you would love to meet or work with, put his picture here.

8 Put a circle of **white flowers** in this sacred space.

9 Take a brick, paint it white, then paint a **powerful word** or expression on it, such as "I believe in miracles" or "good things happen." Put this in your sixth gua.

As far as health is concerned, this gua is associated with your head, skull, and brain. If you suffer from migraines or periodic headaches, improving the energy flow of this area may help. Take a good look at this area of your room and make sure there is no clutter. Also, review the list below and make sure you don't have any of the counterproductive elements in it.

gua 6

What can be in	What should be out
Stuff that reminds you of your dad	Sharp points, triangles
Gray, white, yellow	Red, green
Globes, maps, places you want to visit	STOP signs
Angels, fairies, spirit guides (saints, Buddha figures, etc)	Negative images or images of destruction
Something that reminds you of an important mentor (perhaps a teacher, baby-sitter, camp counselor)	Critics, criticism

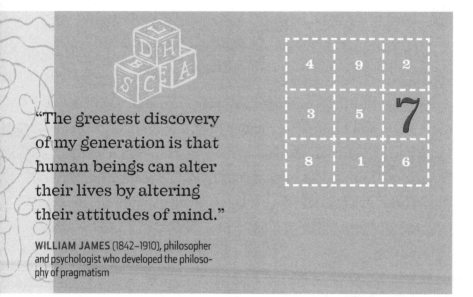

"The greatest discovery of my generation is that human beings can alter their lives by altering their attitudes of mind."

WILLIAM JAMES (1842–1910), philosopher and psychologist who developed the philosophy of pragmatism

GUA 7 Children & Creativity

Have you been working too hard? When people knock on the door and invite you to go play foozball, get a manicure, or watch a movie, do you always say no? Enough with the grindstone! It's time to close the books and **have some fun.** Of course, the opposite is equally true. If you and your friends have established a different theme party for each day of the week, you may want to consider bringing a grounding influence to this gua of your room.

Crystals are one of the best ways to rev up the energy in this gua. Don't feel limited to one kind of crystal: In fact, the spirit of this gua is all about doing things differently from the norm and doing them your own way. Try seeking out small crystal animal figurines or fill a glass jar with big rocks of salt or white bath salts. The idea is to bring **sparkle and light.** The element of this gua is metal, so bring in something brass, gold, silver, or copper — anything that is bright and shiny. What wakes up the little kid inside you? Pez dispensers? Action figures? Crayons and Silly Putty? Whatever it is, bring it here and let your creative spirit know it is playtime.

In the event you find it too hard to study because there is always something fun to do, try to **balance this area** with more weighty or serious objects, such as your dictionary. Take down the wild Japanese paper lanterns you have strung up here and replace them with something more mellow. As always, strive to bring balance to the elements and you will experience good balance in your life.

Solutions to Gua 7

1 This is where you tack up the pictures of **you and your friends** from spring break.

2 Bring in some silly wind-up toys, a yo-yo, a Slinky, or a goofy lunch box.

❸ Create an "idea catcher." Use an old soda can or bottle, a box, a yogurt container . . . anything you've got on hand. Decorate it. **Use your imagination.** When it's done, use it to hold your good ideas.

❹ Hang a poster, photograph, or painting of a lake (best if it has puffy white clouds).

❺ Cut **leaf shapes** out of yellow, orange, and brown construction paper and string them across your window.

❻ Put a metal sculpture on a table or dresser.

❼ Add a gumball machine filled with white gumballs, or put a white stuffed animal in this area.

gua 7

What can be in	What should be out
White	Black, red
Playful, silly objects	Serious, heavy material
Metal (all kinds)	Water, fire
Kids and stuffed animals	Adults and stockbrokers
Karaoke machine	Muzzle

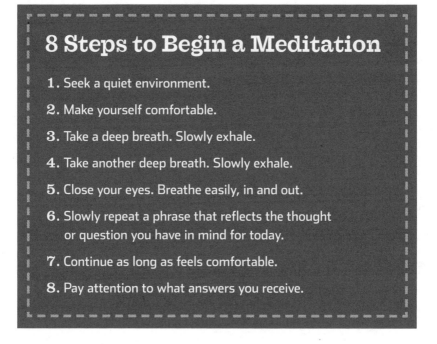

8 Steps to Begin a Meditation

1. Seek a quiet environment.

2. Make yourself comfortable.

3. Take a deep breath. Slowly exhale.

4. Take another deep breath. Slowly exhale.

5. Close your eyes. Breathe easily, in and out.

6. Slowly repeat a phrase that reflects the thought or question you have in mind for today.

7. Continue as long as feels comfortable.

8. Pay attention to what answers you receive.

8 This is where you hang your **glittering disco ball!**

9 Include images of **autumn** on a bright sunny day.

As far as health is concerned, this gua is related to your mouth, teeth, throat, and lungs. It is also symbolic of using your voice and speaking your truth. Perhaps the questionnaire directed you here because you feel blocked in your creativity and in your self-expression. This gua is about coming of age. If you have trouble speaking up for yourself or are extremely shy, give some focus to this area. A little attention on this section of your room will help open up your world dramatically.

4	9	2
3	5	7
8	1	6

"The whole problem with the world is that fools and fanatics are always so certain of themselves, but wiser people so full of doubts."

BERTRAND RUSSELL (1872–1970), one of the founders of analytic philosophy. Russell wrote many spirited antiwar and antinuclear protests.

GUA 8 Knowledge

Sometimes with all the excitement of football games, all-night lounge parties, ultimate Frisbee in the quad, and blogging until after midnight, it's difficult to remember the number one reason that you're in college — that's right, Einstein, you're supposed to be **learning something**. Take a good look at your eighth gua. If things aren't going too well for you academically, chances are this area is blocked, cluttered, or a downright, freaking disaster zone.

No worries: Help is on the way. First, let me talk a little bit about the energy of this gua. This gua is focused on knowledge and self-cultivation. That is to say, it is about going inward to find peace and wisdom. The essence of this area is contemplation, and its element is earth.

When you were a kid, did you like to create sanctuaries for yourself, such as building a cave by draping blankets over chairs, or building forts in the woods, or tucking yourself away in an alcove? If you did, you were following the inclinations of our greatest sages, who have always sought out a peaceful place where they could enjoy uninterrupted contemplation. Why do you think Thoreau was obsessed with Walden Pond? Why did Virginia Woolf insist on a room of one's own? Why did Emily Dickinson never leave her house? (Okay, so maybe Emily took it a little too far . . .) The point is, to develop your mind, you must **cultivate the space and stillness** to hear your own thoughts and to refine them.

Now, let's look at your eighth gua again. Does it reflect peace and quiet or does it have a Nine Inch Nails poster plastered on the wall and a spinning, glittering disco ball? If the gods of perfect dorms are shining on you, you already have your desk set up in this area. As we know all too well, however, sometimes in dorm rooms we have no choice about where to put our desks because someone has already nailed them to the wall for us! But there are ways to work around this.

Solutions for Gua 8

1 Put a big blue or yellow **square pillow** here so that you can sit and meditate.

2 Keep all your books on shelves or in a bookcase.

3 Any and all images of a **mountain** would be excellent here.

4 Images of late winter, especially in hues of a pale, meditative blue, are powerful.

5 Do you know any art students who are doing figure drawing? See whether you can get some of their cast-off sketches of a hand or hands. Put them up here.

6 A small **herb in an earthen pot** would be good here, particularly rosemary or lavender. Or plant seeds with the clear intention for improved inner peace.

7 Add a small **statue of the Buddha.**

8 Place your computer here.

9 Bring in something that is in a very soothing shade of blue, perhaps a scarf or piece of cloth.

As far as health is concerned, this is the area of your hands and back. If you've been having trouble with your back, experiencing backaches or pulled muscles, take a look around this gua. In particular, if you have a lot of your electronics loaded in this space, think about moving them to another location. Also, replace any metal elements with items that are more earthy. For instance, if the chair you have here is wood or metal, try replacing it with a bean bag or a soft, square ottoman. And if you are one of those unlucky types who always seems to have a sprained or broken finger, do some work on this area and perhaps those injuries will become a thing of the past.

gua 8

What can be in	What should be out
Squares, brick, slate	Stereo, telephones, alarm clocks
Soil, anything earthy	Overloaded or overcrowded shelves
Blue, yellow	Green, black, white
Soft rug	Bare cement floors
Diplomas, academic certificates	Disruptive images or sounds
Books	Metal chairs

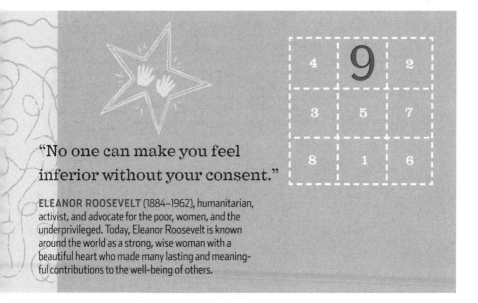

4	9	2
3	5	7
8	1	6

"No one can make you feel inferior without your consent."

ELEANOR ROOSEVELT (1884–1962), humanitarian, activist, and advocate for the poor, women, and the underprivileged. Today, Eleanor Roosevelt is known around the world as a strong, wise woman with a beautiful heart who made many lasting and meaning-ful contributions to the well-being of others.

GUA 9 Fame

If you landed here, chances are you're feeling rather listless about your life in general. People don't seem to know who you are or what you're about. Conversely, you may feel like things are too fired up — you're always on center stage and there's just too much going on and you drink about a gallon of coffee a day to keep up with it all. Take a deep breath. I'm here to help. With some focus, you can develop **inner balance** and have the reputation that best reflects your true self.

There are several aspects to this gua. First and foremost, the ninth gua is about how you are known in the world. It is all about your outer being and how people perceive you. Don't get too hung up on "fame" — it's not really about being famous as much as it is about the community around you and your role in it. If you would like to become more well known, energize this area with an image or a symbol of how you would like to be recognized. Do you dream of the day you will walk down the red carpet and win an Academy Award? Well, make your own Oscar and put it on the shelf here. (I suggest that you wait to practice your acceptance speech until your roomie's in class.)

But let's stay a little closer to home, shall we? Maybe what you want is to look healthier, stronger, smarter, or more confident. Sigh, **don't we all** . . . Here's what you can do: Cut a photo from a magazine that captures the energy and look of how you want to be known and display it in this area. Each day, take a moment to focus on this image and see yourself with these qualities. What kind of photo, you ask? Something that exudes confidence and health. Don't limit yourself to people images and do try to seek something farther afield than advertisements with supermodels. Find pictures and images that are real and vibrant. See whether you can find an animal that is reveling in its natural element or perhaps a landscape that radiates primal life energy. You'll know it when you see it.

A second, very important aspect of this gua is personal integrity. Do you find yourself telling white lies a little too often? Do you feel that people trust you and know that your word is good? If being honest is a struggle for you or you often find yourself compromising your core beliefs, it's time to clear out the fog and bring in the sun! Sunshine is exactly what you need here, particularly as this gua is ruled by the element of fire.

Solutions for Gua 9

1 Place a **red flowering plant** here.

2 If you are allowed candles, this is the ideal spot for them!

3 Paint a **great big sun** and display it here.

4 A bunch of **sunflowers**, especially the red varieties, would power up this area. (Remember, flowers should always be fresh. If you can't get fresh, silk is an acceptable substitute; dried flowers are not.)

5 Shelve here books by people or about people who do what you want to be doing in the future.

6 If you want fame, put **a star** with your name on it here.

7 Get some loose chandelier **crystals** from a secondhand or antiques store and create a mobile to hang in this gua. The crystals will help bring financial rewards for your original ideas.

8 Make or find an oversized letter that is the initial of either your first name or your last (whichever seems more powerful to you) and paint it red, cover it with stars, or put it in lights!

9 Hang up a photograph of a **spectacular sunrise.**

As far as health is concerned, this gua is associated with the eyes and heart. Other vulnerable areas are blood and circulation, the thyroid and glands, and the small intestine. In addition to eye problems and heart attacks, patterns of mental illness and high fevers fall into this area.

gua 9

What can be in	What should be out
Red	Blue
Lava lamp, candles	Water, ice
Light, sunlight	Heavy drapes, shadows
Triangular shapes	Ovals, circles
Images of a volcano	Images of the Arctic Circle

9 More Gua Fixes (for under 99¢)

If you're thinking you need money to make changes happen, get over yourself. Here's a fix for each gua that costs next to nothing, and I'm sure you can think up even more.

Gua	Fix
1	Cut a circle out of white paper and write your ideal job on it with blue ink.
2	Take two chocolate kisses and wrap them up in some red or pink tissue paper and ribbon.
3	Take a box of tissues and paste happy family pictures all over it.
4	Cover a soda can in purple (tissue or paper or paint) and use it as a bank.
5	For three minutes each day, sit in the center of your room, close your eyes, and detach from whatever is causing you stress. Focus on your breath.
6	Create your own personal spirit helper. Use stuff from your desk drawer or whatever you have at hand. Be creative. Add elements with specific intention. When you're done, ask your spirit helper what her name is.
7	Grab some magazines and clip out photos or images of things that bring you joy. Glue or staple these images to bits of cardboard. Take the pieces and make a mobile.
8	Get outside and walk around. Look for a stone that speaks to you. Place it in your 8th gua to represent the mountain triagram. To take it a step further, paint your rock slate blue.
9	Cut a big star out of red paper. Jazz it up with sparkles, glitter, or whatever makes you feel famous!

Particularly Problematic

So maybe right about now you've thrown the bagua across the room in frustration because your room has too many problems that don't seem fixable. Take a breather. Sit back. Put up your feet. Everything's going to be fine. It can seem a bit overwhelming when you begin this, but rest assured: There are cures for everything, and the best cures are always the simplest.

Here's another approach to improving the energy flow in your space. I'm going to take a look at the following aspects of your room: door, windows, beds (including loft and bunk beds), desks, EMFs (electromagnetic fields), and common problem areas. These areas have a critical impact on how well chi moves through your room, so if you make some or all of the adjustments suggested, the chi flow will improve dramatically.

Door

You know what they say about first impressions . . . The door into your room is the gateway to your world. It's one of the most important elements of a room to focus on, so let's take a look at it.

First, you want your door to announce who you are. For example, did you ever notice the front door on the TV show *Friends?* Next time you're watching, check it out. The door is painted purple and there is a whimsical yellow frame around the peephole. Now, I'm not saying you should put curvy little frames on your door if you're not a curvy-little-frame kind of person. The point is that you want your door to **represent you.** Are you fun and whimsical? Studious but kinky? Urban and witty? Country and kicky? Bring your personality to the fore and put it on your door.

Next, if your door is obstructed in any way, you'll feel the constriction in chi flow. For instance, if there's stuff behind the door that keeps it from opening all the way, you may feel that you can never get ahead in life or in your projects because there's always something stuck in your path. This is also true for a rug on the floor that prevents the door from opening smoothly and fully.

In general, you don't want your door to be squeaky or broken. This includes the lock. Even if you don't use the lock, make sure it is fully functional.

Finally, though I know there are often restrictions on how much change you can make to school property, if you can paint your door a color you love, that would be excellent. (**Note:** Don't come crying to me if you get hauled off to the dean's office for drilling holes in your door so you can install a miniature replica of a guillotine at the entranceway. I'm advocating that you use your imagination to enhance your space. Push the boundaries, but don't break 'em. By the way, a guillotine is not really the best message to be sending to the world-at-large, but, hey, whatever floats your boat.) Here's a better approach: A student came back from London with a door-sized poster of a red phone booth which he taped to the door. This not only was whimsical and rather witty, but it also introduced the color red onto the door, which is a very powerful choice.

Windows

Now that you understand the importance of the door, three guesses as to what needs to be done for your windows. That's right (who said you were slow on the uptake?), windows need to be clean, **unobstructed,** and intact.

In feng shui, windows represent your outlook on life. If your windows are dirty, or hidden from view by boxes, or covered up with dark drapes, it wouldn't be a huge surprise to learn that you've been feeling (dare I say it) a wee bit depressed lately. Pull back the shutters and let the sun shine in. Literally. At the bare minimum, for the love of Pete, wash the windows until they're squeaky clean. If there are cracks or breaks in a window, or if it doesn't function as designed, get it fixed ASAP. Got it? Good. Moving on.

Bed

Muy importanto. By now you may be thinking, wait, didn't you say the door and windows were important? Come on — what isn't important for crying out loud?!

Not to worry. Of course it's all important. Think of your body. Would you say your toes are less important than your lungs for

running a race? Of course not. It's all of a piece, so stay with me. I was discussing your bed.

The best position for your bed is to have the headboard **against a solid wall** and for the door to be visible to you from the bed, although you don't want your bed to be directly facing the door.

Ha, you say. As if you have any choice. Well, if you can't put your bed into the optimal position, try these work-arounds.

If your headboard is not against a wall, create support behind your head with a piece of furniture or some large pillows.

If your bed is facing the door, place a bookcase or bureau at the foot of the bed to provide protection from the door.

What about loft beds, you ask? Well, like anything else, they have their good points and their not-so-good points. Obviously, lofting your bed gives you more floor space and improves the living area of your dorm room. It's key, however, that you build a solid loft. Beds should not be wobbly or on wheels. (Jeez — don't tell me you have a loft on wheels! Stop that noise.) When you focus on your bed, the word you want to use is grounded. The more stable your bed, the more stable your life.

Here's a suggestion to "ground" your loft bed, but I'm pretty sure you can come up with an even better idea, you creative genius. Paint the frame and legs of your loft bed dark brown (like a tree trunk) and add leaves or vines. The idea (for those of you reading this at 4 A.M. and too tired to make the connection) is to root the bed symbolically into the ground.

Now for the dreaded bunk bed. The issues facing a person who sleeps in a bunk bed depends on whether she has the top bunk or the bottom. For the top-bunker, the biggest issue is headroom. It's not advisable to sleep just inches from the ceiling, but I understand that sometimes you have no choice (I'm very understanding that way). If the space is tight, put something on the ceiling that will expand the space. A common (and good) choice is to create the illusion of a night sky. Anything that creates a sense of dimension will help this.

If you're the lucky winner of the bottom bunk, your challenge is having all that weight over your head while you sleep. The result is often a feeling that things are pressing down on you or that you can never be free of heavy thoughts. An easy but effective cure for the bottom-bunker is to hang a small, round, faceted crystal (10 mm) at the head and foot of the bed (if crystals aren't easy to come by, feathers will work equally well). This will lighten the energy and help the chi flow.

No matter what bed type you sleep in, pay attention to the linens you use. Ideally, your sheets are **clean and soft** to the touch. Rough, cheap materials will give you rough, cheap sleep. If you're someone who does laundry only every six weeks, have more than one set of sheets (your roommate will thank you!). Do not use a sleeping bag instead of sheets; we're not camping here. As far as colors go, sheets should be rather cool and calming. Neutrals are good, as are pale blues and greens. If you opt for very active colors, such as bright red and burning yellow, expect to see a whole lot more activity in your bed than sleep (and that's all I'm going to say on the matter).

Desk

In the same way that your bed should be positioned to support you, the desk needs to be situated so that you can **do your best** in school. (For those of you who may have forgotten, college was intended to be an academic environment, not simply a really great way to meet cool people.) The best desk position is where you sit with a view of the door, with a solid wall behind your back.

Yeah, right. My desk is screwed to the wall, you say. Well, you're not alone. Unfortunately, dorm interior design is sorely lacking a feng shui influence. But never fear. Here's one fix: If when you're sitting at your desk you can't see the door, place a small mirror above the desk so that it reflects the door. This little trick can do wonders for your chi.

Aside from placement, the best thing you can do for your desk is to keep it clean and free of clutter. To prevent pileups, clear the desktop once a week. This will give you a fresh start and a fresh perspective on your studies. Try it for a couple of weeks. You'll see. (I know you don't want to believe me, but it'll make a big difference and then you'll be glad you read this book and all will be right with the world! Well, maybe.)

EMFs

Whaaaaaat? UFOs? No, dummy. EMFs. Electromagnetic fields. If you're not already aware of them, let me explain. All of your electronic equipment (clock radio, computer, printer, stereo, VCR, DVD player, refrigerator, microwave, cell phone, hair dryer, curling iron, lights . . .) emit electric fields and magnetic fields. As long as an electric cord is plugged in, an electric field is active. Magnetic fields are active once a device is turned on.

What, you may ask, has this to do with anything?

The answer is that no one knows. It may be years before we know the impact of EMFs on our health. (This book is oh-so obviously not about EMFs, so if you want more info, please head to the last section, References and Recommended Reading.) My point is simply that if you have even half of the items listed above in your small dorm room, you are getting blitzed with EMFs. Try to bring your attention to this and modify some behavior to prevent health issues such as headaches, dizziness, rashes, and fatigue. Don't go to sleep with your TV running or the lights on or the stereo blasting. Turn off as much electronic equipment as possible before going to sleep. Then tune in to how you feel in a few weeks — chances are you'll feel calmer and less wound up.

Help, you cry out! I can't possibly live without my stereo, my TV, my computer, my hair dryer (you'll have to pull my hair dryer from my cold, dead hands), my refrigerator, my . . . Stop. I hear you. No one is suggesting you ditch your stuff. I'm just trying to make you aware of its presence and its influence on your life energy. And, as always, there are cures.

A terrific way to lower the electronic frequencies in your room is to bring in green plants. Healthy green plants help absorb EMFs and toxins in the air. Particularly good choices are philodendrons, peace lilies, and palm plants. Place the plants close to your electronic equipment and be sure to keep them fed and watered.

Now, let's review.

Clock radio Although most people place their clock radios next to their head, I'm advising that you break 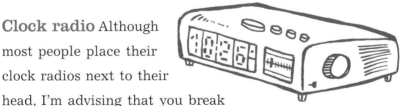 with the pack and move it as far away as possible. Some clock radios emit high electromagnetic frequencies. If you must have the alarm close at hand, switch to a windup clock or one that runs on batteries.

Microwave and refrigerator Since  when did dorm rooms become kitchenettes, anyway? The best thing is not to have either appliance in your space. If you insist, however, try to place them both far from where you sleep and study. Don't have either pointing directly at you.

Computer and printer I'm about to change some bad behavior here. Raise your hand if you don't turn these off before you go to bed. Just as I thought. Most people leave them running. Don't be like most people. If you want the best sleep, shut them off and unplug them. When you are sleeping, the best place for electronics is behind closed doors or covered up. Because you may not have a closed cabinet in which to store your computer and printer, cover them with a beautiful cloth when they are not in use. This small practice will do wonders to shift the energies in your space.

TV By now you can guess what I'm going to say about having a TV in your dorm room (besides the obvious question: Isn't it rather distracting to be watching reruns when you have an exam to study for?). Keep the TV a good distance — at least three feet — away from you. The farther away from the TV you sit, the less likely that EMFs will affect you.

Stereo As with all of your other electronics, keep out of the direct path of your stereo and DVD player. Do play lots of music: Music brings in rocking chi and can shift energy that is stale and stagnant. Not to make any judgments here, but FYI, classical music is best for lifting chi; the vibrations are higher than that of rock and roll. And rock and roll emits higher vibrations than rap. You can do more investigation of this phenomenon on your own, and there's lots of information available on the Internet.

Common Problem Areas

Trash can I'm going to talk about your trash can. Do you think I'm going just a little bit over the top? Well, I'm not. This is one of the most common ways to foul up your chi flow, and the simple truth is that it is by far the easiest thing to remedy. Don't let your trash build up and overflow. Empty your trash every day; otherwise, you may feel that there's a lot of garbage and guff messing up your life. So get rid of it. Do the literal and watch the figurative follow suit.

Pictures and posters Be thoughtful about what you put up on your walls. If you're feeling a bit jumbled and not sure of just who you are these days, take a look around your room and see what's on the walls. Is there a wide range of images that clash? (Obviously, I would never suggest that you be a narrow person with just one side to your personality. Be real.) What I'm trying to ask is, is there a common thread among the images? Do they support and enhance one another or are they sharply contrasting to the point of visual cacophony?

Use pictures and posters to support and increase the energies that you want to bring into your life. For instance, if you'd like to be doing better with your schoolwork, maybe take down

 a couple of the raucous Oktoberfest banners and replace them with something a bit more contemplative. On the other hand, if you feel that you've always got your nose to the grindstone and never seem to be having any fun, take down that life-size black-and-white poster of Schopenhauer and hang a brightly colored piñata in its place. As always, strive for balance. If you feel your room is listing to one side, bring in elements that will restore the equilibrium.

Closets One of the biggest misconceptions is that if someone can't see how messy something is, it doesn't really count. Yeah, right. With that logic, downing a candy bar doesn't add calories if no one sees you eat it. Honestly. Go over to your closet right now. Can you open the door? Is the door always half open because you can't get it shut? Does it seem crammed to the gills with stuff, but you never seem to be able to find the right shoes or the perfect outfit?

Face it. This dorm room and this dorm closet provide you with limited space. You've got to deal with that reality. So if you've got a closet that is out of control, you need to take charge and whip it into shape. The first thing you want to do is empty it out. ALL of it. Then, sort everything into two piles: Love it, can't live without it; never use it, never wear it. If you don't use or wear something very often, you can't afford to keep it around. All this extra stuff will drag you down. If you have to keep it but aren't using it now, send it home. Otherwise, give it away. Now.

Clear your space. When you do start putting things back into your closet, do so with a thought to organization. Make your stuff easily accessible.

Storage bins Sometimes we go overboard with storage bins, and our room looks like an aisle in Wal-Mart. Storage bins are

a great solution to keeping things contained and organized, but not if they are crowding you out of your room. Once stuff goes into a bin, don't think you never have to empty it again. Bins shouldn't be functioning as permanent wastebaskets. Go through the storage bins on at least a quarterly basis and make sure you are not holding on to stuff that should be moved out. The best thing you can do is have *less* stuff. That is how you will have more energy and stronger chi in both your room and your life.

Dressers and bureaus Follow the guidelines I laid out for your closet and you'll be in the clear. A simple rule of thumb is that all drawers should open easily and close completely. If your drawers are crammed with stuff to the point that you can't pull them open, let alone access half of what's jammed in there, make a change. Dump out the drawers and purge everything you don't love and can live without. Then restore order.

The top of your dresser is also an area to review. Do you have stuff spilling out all over it? Clear it off. Keep it neat and clean. I may be sounding like your mother right about now (**Note:** I am not your mother), but truly, these changes will smooth out the energies and you will notice a difference.

Under your bed Come on, don't even try to fake me out with "There's so little room in my dorm and that's why there's so much crap under my bed." I know you've always had crap under your bed. Let's be honest. The fact is, there shouldn't be anything under your bed, including dust bunnies. Yet I do understand (because, as I've said before, I'm really understanding that way) that dorm rooms require maximizing all  available space. So if you're going to put stuff under the bed, make sure it's not just dirty laundry. Use the space for storage bins that are neatly placed and pulled out often enough that they don't get covered in so much dust that they look like they've spent years in a crypt.

Bookshelves One word of caution on shelving. Make sure shelves are securely fastened to the wall or, if they are on the floor, that they are a stable unit. If you can avoid it, don't put shelves above your bed. You don't want a potential accident hovering over you as you sleep. And last, be smart. Keep the heavier books on the bottom and the lighter volumes on top.

 Knickknacks and tchotchkes Otherwise known as clutter. Just what is all this crap you've got everywhere? Get it gone. It's taking up space and slowing down your chi. Clear it out.

Messy roommates Oh boy. Do I hear you: "What difference does it make that I've taken care of my side when my roomie is

trying to win a place in the *Guinness Book of World Records* for largest disaster area ever created by a single person?" There's no easy solution to this problem. Having said that, however, if you keep thinking that your roomie is a total slob, you will feed that reality. Try to envision living with a roommate who keeps her half of the room up to par. Perhaps your roomie will be influenced by how you keep your side. Perhaps your roomie will decide to move out and a new roomie will come in who is a better fit for you. Anything is possible. Keep your intention focused on what you want and see it as if it has already come true.

Feng Shui and the Health/Body Connection

Feng shui is not a replacement for medical solutions. If you are sick, or think you are sick, seek medical attention. Follow the advice given by your doctor or other health practitioner.

What I want to bring to your attention is that feng shui can help you create an environment that supports your health, brings **peace of mind,** and nurtures your spirit. By improving the energy flow of your living space, you may easily find the right doctors or other healers and get the proper medical care when you need it.

Cures for Common Ailments

Here are some common ailments and feng shui suggestions for bringing balance. It goes without saying that you should clear all clutter and make sure that everything is in proper working order, the electricity and plumbing included. (Leaky plumbing can have an adverse effect on health and welfare, particularly when it is centrally located.)

Ailment	Gua	Helped by	Hindered by
Headaches	6: Helpful People & Travel	Earth, metal	Water, wood, fire
Backaches	8: Knowledge	Fire, earth	Metal, water, wood
Stomach ailments	2: Relationships 5: The Center	Fire, earth	Metal, water, wood
Foot problems	3: Family	Water, wood	Fire, earth, metal
Heart troubles	9: Fame	Wood, fire	Earth, metal, water
Earaches	1: Career	Metal, water	Wood, fire, earth
Respiratory problems	4: Prosperity	Water, wood	Fire, earth, metal
Mouth, teeth, lungs	7: Creativity & Children	Earth, metal	Wood, fire
Eye disorders	9: Fame	Wood, fire	Earth, metal, water

Health & Body Connection

Gua 4 **Prosperity** Hips, legs, buttocks, pelvis, small bones, respiration	Gua 9 **Fame** Eyes, heart, circulation, glands, small intestine, mental illness, high fevers	Gua 2 **Relationships** Stomach, spleen, immune system, digestive problems
Gua 3 **Family** Feet, liver, big bones, gallbladder, hysteria, phobias	Gua 5 **Center** Overall health & well-being	Gua 7 **Children & Creativity** Lungs, mouth, teeth, colon, skin, throat, large intestine
Gua 8 **Knowledge** Fingers, hands, back, shoulders, spine, constipation	Gua 1 **Career** Ears, kidneys, bladder, bodily fluids, reproductive system	Gua 6 **Helpful People & Travel** Head, skull, brain, migraine headaches

Power of Intention

Living in the same small space with another person can test the patience of even a saint. And you're no saint. So what are you gonna do?

Remember, the most important tool you've got is intention. Even if you're certain that your current roommate is the spawn of aliens, your behavior is what will change the situation. Which is a good thing, because it's really your only option and the only thing you have the power to change.

Typical problems between roommates stem from pronounced differences. Either she's the neat freak and you're the slob, or she's having her friends over for a group pedicure when you're trying to read Nietzsche. Whatever the specifics, the solution lies in **how you set boundaries.** And here's where feng shui can help you come up with some sweet solutions.

Because there isn't enough room to sneeze, you've got to get creative. The physical boundaries you might want to create — such as an airtight, opaque fiberglass wall down the middle of the room — are really just metaphors for the internal boundaries you need to develop to have a good roomie relationship.

The cool thing is that once you've made the changes in the room, you can forget about them and they'll work on their own, while you're at class, sleeping through class, playing video games, or vegging with friends. For real!

On your desk, put a picture of you and someone you love (preferably someone you've actually met). You can also use your

Chinese natal animals to impart your individual energy by choosing enhancements that have that energy. (See pages 108–123 for details.) For example, if you are a Rat, you love things that are bizarre and exotic. String up some Tibetan prayer flags and see what the energy brings.

How will this change anything? The trick is to use this dorky (but useful) mnemonic: the three Cs — current, cared for, and contained.

The nature of chi is to be **lively and flowing**, like a skilled social butterfly. If it's not refreshed by use, it gets bored and stale and just can't resist inviting in the first thing that comes along. So clear off the notes from last semester (which you never studied anyway), ditch the *People* magazine you've had since Thanksgiving, and, well — you get the idea. Keep it current.

Now the biggie: You must care for your chi. If it looks like you don't care about your stuff, why would anyone else? Chi doesn't like to be ignored. Neglected chi sulks in the corner and tends to send bad vibes to everyone.

Last, if you want boundaries, make boundaries. It's up to you to contain your stuff. Leaving your hair straightener on your roomie's desk because it's closer to the outlet compromises the boundary line. **It's a two-way street.** If your shoes are invading the space in front of her bed, don't be surprised when some of her stuff starts sliding into your space.

Now, for some real-life roomie situations, let's go into some before-and-afters.

Before & After

Are you ready to see some feng shui in action? Good deal. Here are some before-and-after case studies done by Elizabeth, Peg, and myself, of people just like you — dorm dwellers. It goes without saying that all names have been changed to protect the privacy of our guinea pigs, uh, our helpful participants. So if you happen to know anybody in college named Jen, Amy, Josh, Jacqueline, Sophie, or Tom, don't be confused: He or she is not one of the people featured here because the people here are not really named Jen, Amy, Josh, Jacqueline, Sophie, and Tom. Sheesh. Some people need everything spelled out for them.

With any luck, some of the issues these students deal with may be the same as or similar to issues you face. Our hope is that this will be useful to you as well as informative.

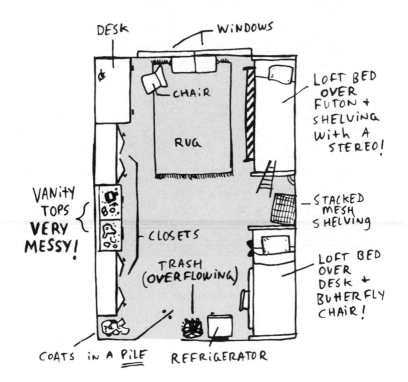

DESK

WINDOWS

CHAIR

LOFT BED OVER FUTON + SHELVING with A STEREO!

RUG

VANITY TOPS VERY MESSY!

STACKED MESH SHELVING

CLOSETS

TRASH (OVERFLOWING)

LOFT BED OVER DESK + BUTERFLY CHAIR!

COATS IN A PILE   REFRIGERATOR

Room #1: Jen

Jen is a sophomore. She shares her room with Amy, who was willing to allow Jen to make any changes to the room as needed. Here are the results of Jen's questionnaire: Relationships, Helpful People, and Knowledge guas emerged as "high importance" areas. Jen reported frequent stomach problems (Relationships), a strained relationship with her dad (Helpful People), occasional headaches (Helpful People), feeling academically challenged (Knowledge), and struggling with classes (Knowledge).

Jen and Amy both indicated that they were feeling a lot of stress, that they weren't as calm as they used to be, and that they felt as if the clutter in their room was getting out of control. They both spoke about particular fears, and each was having trouble staying focused on classes. Both students also felt that their quality of sleep could use some improvement.

What Is Out of Balance in Room #1?

After a review of their room, the two most critical issues contributing to their problems were 1) they both slept in very vulnerable positions and 2) they had way too much stuff packed into their tiny dorm room. These co-eds definitely brought more "home" with them than they needed. The vanity tops were covered with lotions, potions, hair clips, jewelry, cosmetics, and photos. The drawers and closets were jammed with enough clothes and shoes to outfit all of the Miss America contestants for, oh, say, about *ten years*. The trash can was overflowing to the point that the corner in which it sat was the trash *area*. Candy bar wrappers and soda cans were simply tossed in the general direction of the can.

If the roomies didn't have enough problems with the tsunami of clutter that threatened to drown them, their room was also overloaded with electronics. Two clock radios sat right by Amy's head when she slept at night. Amy's desk chair was directly beside the refrigerator, so as she studied, the little electronic beast pointed straight at her stomach. As you learned in the Particularly Problematic section (page 68), EMFs are to be avoided. (Don't tell me you skipped that section; you're breakin' my heart!)

To their credit, Jen and Amy had done a lot to decorate their room in a fun, upbeat way. Tiny white lights were strung across the ceiling. Whimsical pieces were added here and there with very personal flair. Both roomies professed to love their room.

What the young women didn't realize was that some of their creative features were actually to blame for the discomfort they were experiencing. For example, both beds were lofted, but the bed frames were metal and they appeared somewhat unstable. (Remember, solid wooden bed frames are the best choice for a sound sleep and the best sleeping position is where you can see the door but are not directly in front of it, and preferably where you have a wide view of the room.)

Neither student was sleeping in a **command position.** Without headboards on the beds, each had little support. They were sleeping with the crown of their heads pointing toward the door, the reverse of what is recommended. To make matters worse, Amy slept with her head by Jen's feet. In addition, it looked like a warehouse for Circuit City under Jen's bed: two computers, a printer, a stereo, and a refrigerator. All they were missing was a subzero freezer and a satellite dish.

Did they actually expect to get any SLEEP in this place?!

Before   **After**

THE BIG FIX for Room #1

First, Jen wrote down her top three intentions — that is, what she most wanted to see come into her life. She wrote her intentions in the present tense, as if they were happening now. Then she tucked her intentions into a special place. Next, Jen followed our oh-so-gentle suggestions.

 Clear the clutter.

2 Clear the bureau tops. Wash them down and put *everything* away. (The vanities were located in the Family gua, so clearing them created room for family issues to be clarified and for ties to be strengthened.)

3 Relocate the refrigerator.

 Paint the loft frame brown.

5 Turn off the computers at night before sleeping and cover them with a beautiful cloth.

6 Place seven ribbons, one for each color of the rainbow (red, orange, yellow, green, blue, indigo, purple), on the inside of their doorknob.

7 Change the futon cover, which was blue and white striped to pink or yellow (colors for relationships).

8 Replace the blue snowflakes on the window with big red hearts, for both recognition and relationships.

Jen's Room AFTER

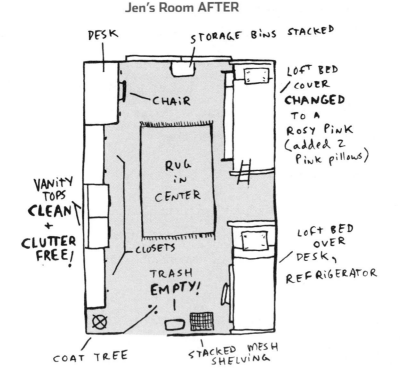

DESK

STORAGE BINS STACKED

CHAIR

LOFT BED / COVER CHANGED TO A ROSY PINK (added 2 PINK pillows)

RUG iN CENTER

VANITY TOPS CLEAN + CLUTTER FREE!

CLOSETS

LOFT BED OVER / DESK, REFRIGERATOR

TRASH EMPTY!

COAT TREE

STACKED MESH SHELVING

9 Begin a daily "OM" practice. Meditation is a great way to focus intention, strengthen chi, and become more grounded. As you **clear your "inside" clutter,** you open yourself to creativity, opportunity, options, and solutions.

As Jen made these changes, she was instructed to follow the Three Secrets Reinforcement (see page 133) and to visualize the result. (**Note:** Visualizing the result and believing it will happen are significant parts of attracting what you want into your life.)

TA-DAAAAHHHHH! (Er, Ahem: The Results)

Jen's primary intention was to improve her relationships. She wanted deep friendships but she also wanted to get better at making true friends with guys. She changed the futon cover from blue and white stripes to a pretty pink. She also brought in some pink pillows and jazzed up the lamp.

To become more grounded, Jen painted the lofted bed frame to resemble a tree trunk. Both roomies loved it and said it made a huge difference. The beds gave the illusion of being lower to the ground and the women no longer felt that they were floating in the air. Interestingly enough, even though the beds felt better, Jen began to sleep on the futon, in the Relationships area. This put her in a position of strength . . . with a solid wall behind her and a view of the door. She slept great there, so she continued to sleep on the futon for the rest of the semester.

Also, the clutter was gone. Both roomies gave away clothes they no longer wore, packed up sweaters and sent them home, and got rid of excess knickknacks. They even gave away the butterfly chair that was crowded into Amy's study area. The refrigerator was moved. A beautiful crystal was hung from the ceiling in the center of the room, and (GASP... be sure you're sitting to read this next part) *they began to empty the trash can regularly.* They also played around with color, enhancing the various areas of the bagua with the tones that support each one.

Jen reported that her relationships transformed in significant ways after making these modifications to her room. However, in order for new relationships to come in, some of her existing relationships broke off. As Jen put it, several relationships "cracked." She felt betrayed by certain friends and hurt by others. But all the while, she was feeling exhilarated because her life was moving in a new direction and those relationships would have held her back. Jen realized that she was undergoing some big life changes that her friends weren't. She will have a different roommate for the following year and will live in another dormitory. She's looking forward to building friendships that fit in with the ways she has grown and developed.

Jen's relationship with her dad, which had been strained for many months, made meaningful progress. This was one of Jen's three intentions. She also says she is making friends with guys more easily. You go, girl!

As Jen learned, feng shui is not a magic bullet whereby everything is positive and you never have any problems. Sometimes, negative things happen before better situations emerge. Jen is philosophical about her situation. She knows that she is transforming faster than are those around her. Although it's not always the most comfortable situation, she is able to keep it in perspective. She says she is looking forward to beginning her junior year on solid ground.

Recycling Your Clutter

- **Choose a day or an evening** to gather up and get rid of your excess stuff. Celebrate your new space with friends.

- **Bring your excess stuff** to the local thrift shop or Goodwill.

- **Get a digital camera** and take photos of the stuff you want to get rid of. Then post them on eBay and see what sells.

- If your campus doesn't have an exchange center, **create one!** This could be a wonderful service project!

- **Give your excess stuff to a local charity or church.** See whether the charity is having a tag sale to make money, then donate your belongings to the cause.

- **Throw a gift exchange party** in your dorm after the holidays. Ask everyone to bring something they don't want and can't exchange. Your trash is sure to be someone's treasure!

Room #2: Josh

Josh is a freshman in a double room. Intrigued about feng shui, he decided to give it a try. When asked to describe himself, Josh said he is a very private person and not prone to outward displays of affection. Josh was honest enough to share that he has a tendency to be sarcastic and critical. He experiences periodic headaches, procrastinates more than he cares to, and would like to be more organized.

Josh's Room BEFORE

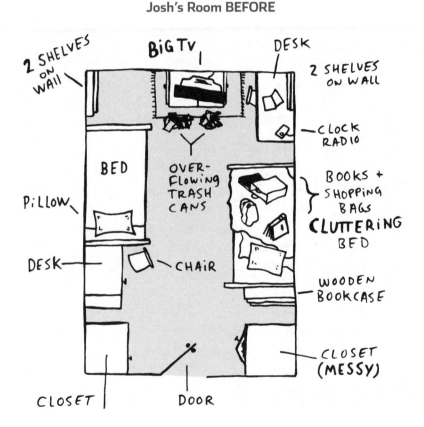

After filling out the 3-Minute Questionnaire, Josh's key areas of concentration ended up being Helpful People, Knowledge, and the Center.

A quick analysis of Josh's room reveals a rather classic "my side vs. your side" setup. Unlike Jen and Amy, who had made a room that was "ours," Josh and his roommate had clearly **defined boundary lines.** Each side had a closet, a bed, a desk, a chair, and a bureau. The left side of the room belonged to Josh's roommate, but because he wasn't participating, we stayed away from there. We focused our attention on the right side of the room.

The first thing we noticed was that Josh's closet, located to the right of the door, was in the Helpful People gua (the area that rules the head). We opened the door to his closet to discover a disaster zone. Uh, hello, Sherlock? Clean the closet and reduce the headaches? Could it be that simple? We'll see . . .

What Is Out of Balance in Room #2?

Josh slept with the top of his head pointing toward the door (and even you know by now that's a no-no). Was Josh getting a **good night's sleep?** Of course not.

Overall, Josh's room was small and stark. White walls. A couple of Red Sox posters and a trophy from his high school baseball tournament. (What would *Queer Eye* say?!) Although there wasn't much in the way of clutter, his books and sports gear were unceremoniously dumped on the floor. Luckily for

Josh, his roommate was a neat freak. One consequence is that the roomie's spic-and-span closet is located in the Knowledge gua, which has a positive effect on Josh's academics.

One thing Josh emphasized was that he wasn't interested in making big, visible changes. He preferred that the changes be subtle. (And we, being utterly adaptable, did precisely what he requested.) We made small suggestions for just a few specific areas in his room. And, we brought his attention to the colors he chose to wear and have around him.

THE BIG FIX for Room #2

Here's what we asked Josh to do:

1 Turn around in his bed, so he can see the door.

2 Shut off the electronics when sleeping. Move his clock away from his head.

Before   After

3 Clear out the clutter from under his bed.

4 Empty the trash daily.

5 Clean his closet. Take everything out, wipe it down, and put everything back neatly. Ditch all nonessentials.

6 Place a mirror by his desk to see the door.

7 Wear earthy colors such as brown, orange, and yellow to ground himself on the days he's feeling unorganized and all over the place. (Bonus points: It turns out that Josh loves orange! Who knew?) Wear "metal" colors, such as white and gray, to help cut right through things and get to the point. Wear "water" colors, such as black and navy blue, on the days he is feeling too sarcastic, too analytical, too sharp. (Water colors soften you, doncha know.)

TA-DAAAAHHHHH!

Josh reversed his sleeping position and began sleeping so that he faced the door: In other words, he could see the door from his pillow. He also cleared out under his bed. Within a week he called to report that (surprise, surprise) his sleep improved and that he was not getting as many headaches.

As for his struggle with procrastination, one time we spoke he was just beginning a project (due the following day, natch) that he had had *all semester to do.* Because he is very skilled in pulling the all-nighter, Josh got it done in record time. But a few

Josh's Room AFTER

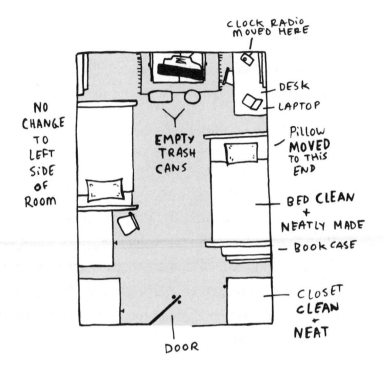

CLOCK RADIO MOVED HERE

DESK

LAPTOP

NO CHANGE TO LEFT SIDE OF Room

EMPTY TRASH CANS

Pillow MOVED TO THIS END

BED CLEAN + NEATLY MADE

BOOKCASE

CLOSET CLEAN + NEAT

DOOR

weeks later, once the feng shui fixes were well under way, Josh called to say he was feeling great about a very difficult exam. This time, rather than wait until the last minute, he began studying a week and a half ahead of time. Procrastination was one of the issues he had hoped to improve by addressing the chi energy in his room, and in his words, "It [the procrastination] just fell by the wayside when it came time to prepare for this exam." When we asked what changes he had made, Josh said he had cleared out everything from under his bed (everything except his stash of bottled water) and he was making an effort to keep the top of his bureau clean.

One other tip. Josh replaced his pillowcases with bright red ones. Red is a great color for getting rid of procrastination. (Bear in mind, however, that if you have attention deficit disorder or find it difficult to concentrate, red is not recommended.)

Get Your Green Thumb On

Plants are great chi enhancers in your Family, Prosperity, and Fame guas. If you have too much of the earth, metal, or water element, add a plant. It will help balance out the energy.

Jade and bamboo plants are often recommended for feng shui cures, and these are both excellent in the Prosperity area. However, there are lots of other plants to choose from that bring good energies. Here are some: areca palm, bamboo palm, rubber plant, dracaena ('Janet Craig' variety), English ivy, Boston fern, peace lily, corn plant, ficus (also known as a weeping fig), and schefflera. Each of these plants has a high rating for removing chemical vapors and is relatively easy to care for. See below for more information on growing a feng shui friendly houseplant.

Follow your instincts when selecting a plant. Choose it because you love it. Don't put a plant in your environment if it looks or feels out of place.

☞ Avoid plants that have **sharp, bladelike leaves.**

☞ Don't purchase a plant that looks **droopy or sad.**

☞ It is important to keep your plant **healthy and clean.** Remove dead leaves and don't let dust accumulate.

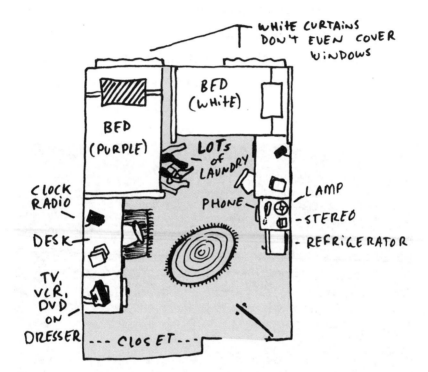

Room #3: Sophie & Jacqueline

Sophie and Jacqueline are sophomore women who share a room within a dorm suite. A total of seven women live in the four-room suite.

Interestingly, the results of Jacqueline and Sophie's questionnaires were identical except for one area. Jacqueline's questionnaire highlighted Career, Family, Knowledge, and Fame.

Sophie's was the same but she also had highlighted the Relationships gua. Both students reported experiencing anxiety and frequent health imbalances.

One thing that Jacqueline and Sophie had going for them was that all of their furniture was freestanding. It goes without saying (but I'll say it anyway, because I love to be difficult) that the more freedom you have in how you place your furniture, the better your chances of **optimizing the flow of chi.**

The roommates tended to change the furniture around a lot, but when we worked with them, Jacqueline was living on the left side of the room and Sophie was living on the right. We noticed right away that the entryway was small and congested. And the two women shared one closet that had no door, so everything was out in the open and could be viewed from the room. Hmmm, are you thinking what we were thinking? Uh-huh, that closet definitely needs attention.

What Is Out of Balance in Room #3?

It was a funny mix. On the one hand, both Jacqueline and Sophie are very creative, so their room was extremely arty. On the other hand, their space was stuffed to the gills with, well, stuff. The closet was packed, and a peek under the beds revealed still more stuff.

No wonder both these *chicas* had issues with anxiety. Where's the chi gonna settle down and have a nice cup of tea in a place like this?

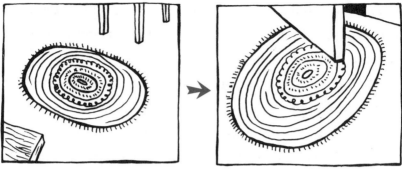

Before   **After**

THE BIG FIX for Room #3

Here's a few suggestions we gave to Jacqueline and Sophie:

 Jacqueline and Sophie should write down their intentions in the present tense, just as if they were happening now.

 Sophie needs to move the clock radio away from her head.

❸ Place a curtain or beautiful fabric over the closet to serve as a door. This will really help quiet things down.

 Move the rectangular rug into the center of the room.

❺ Move the oval rug to the entryway.

❻ Get curtains to fit the windows or use scarves for fun energy.

❼ Add some red to help activate the Fame gua.

❽ Jacqueline should place a mirror by her desk to enable her to view the door.

9 Reinforce all changes using the Three Secrets Reinforcement (see page 133).

Sophie & Jacqueline's Room AFTER

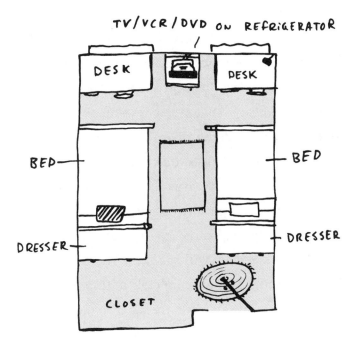

TA-DAAAAHHHHH!

There was no spare cash to make any purchases, so Sophie and Jacqueline took an alternate route. They rearranged their room. They made it more symmetrical, so that as you entered, the bureaus were close to the door, followed by their beds, followed by their desks. One interesting note: Both women slept with their head pointing toward the door. Not the recommended approach, but they said they slept better this way. And in this case, their dressers were acting as headboards, which provided solid support. Because results are what matter, go with what works best for you. It's okay to modify the rules and suggestions we provide here.

Within weeks, Sophie reported that things were going extremely well for her. She was feeling happier with her design projects and her grades. She said she was feeling less stressed out and at work she'd even gotten a raise in pay. Go figure!

Jacqueline was also doing well, although her knees were giving her some problems. Knees (like the legs and hips) are associated with the Prosperity area, but her classes were going smoothly. We provided some more suggestions to boost her Prosperity gua, which she will carry forward into her junior year.

Jacqueline and Sophie will share the same room next year. They cleaned out their room completely at the end of the semester and said they are eager to get a fresh start in the fall, and will apply the feng shui techniques that they've learned. Over the summer they will look for curtains and for a beautiful cloth to cover their closet door.

9 More Gua Fixes (for under 99¢)

The trick to feng shui fixes is setting your intention around change. If you're having trouble coming up with an easy fix for each gua, try one of these.

Gua	Fix
1	Keep a small bowl of water in this area. Freshen the water daily.
2	Make two hearts out of red or pink construction paper. Attach them and place here.
3	Draw a picture of a sunrise to represent a new day and new beginnings.
4	List 27 blessings in your life or things for which you are grateful. Put in an envelope here.
5	Hang a miniature globe from the ceiling in the center of the room. You can make one using a tennis ball, paper, and colored markers.
6	Take a small rock and make a power stone, an angel stone, or a spirit stone. You can draw on it, paint it, write power words . . . whatever your heart desires.
7	Draw a picture of a beautiful sunset to represent rest and relaxation — just what you need after a long day of studying.
8	Create a mountain out of small rocks or pebbles. Glue them together and place a stick figure of yourself on the summit of the mountain. Make your stick figure out of toothpicks or pipe cleaners or whatever you have around.
9	Cut a picture out of a magazine that represents what you plan to do with your life and how you want to be known. Hang it in this area.

Room #4: Tom

Tom shares a room with two other guys. He is the only one participating in using feng shui to improve his space. This room is divided into three sections. Each student has his own area. As it happens, Tom is in the most vulnerable position in the room,

Tom's Room BEFORE

so he needs the help more than his roomies do, because they both occupy positions of strength and are fairly well protected.

To start with, Tom studies with his back to the door and sleeps close to the door. Tom's area occupies the left side of the room just as you enter. His area covers the Knowledge, Family, and Prosperity guas. (Roomie #2 is happily tucked away in the Relationships corner, and Roomie #3 is hidden from view in the Helpful People and Career guas.) Oh yeah, the TV and DVD occupy the Fame gua.

What Is Out of Balance in Room #4?

One thing Tom loves about this room is that he has a lot more space than he had at home. For him, the room feels more open and spacious than what he is used to. He did mention, however, that he would like to be farther away from the door. (Kudos to Tom on his highly functioning intuition.) It *should* feel uncomfortable to be so close to the door, because that is one of the most vulnerable positions to be in.

Another issue for Tom is that he's frequently broke. He would like to have more money so he can travel and visit his girlfriend. (Tom lives on the East Coast and his girlfriend lives on the West Coast.) He also said he would like to be less of a procrastinator and have more close friends.

THE BIG FIX for Room #4

Tom's action plan included the following:

1 Turn around and sleep facing the door. Although Tom couldn't move his bed, turning around would put his head farther away from the door.

2 Move the clock radio away from his head. (Do we get tired of telling people this? Never!) Move all electronics as far away as possible from his head when he is sleeping.

3 Place a mirror by the desk to provide a view of the door.

4 Clear the desktop at least weekly. This will help reduce procrastination.

5 Sit outside of the path of the microwave. (Not only was Tom sitting directly across from the door, but his study position was directly across from the microwave as well — it's a lucky thing we came to the rescue.)

6 Tom would like more money. And the boy hit the lottery. Not the real lottery, of course, but even though his position in the room was largely unfortunate, the Prosperity gua was in his space. Thus, he can influence this area and activate its energy. Tom was asked to clear all clutter, place a green plant on the windowsill, and set an intention for money flowing in easily and effortlessly. Tom was also asked to visualize his perfect summer job and to focus an intention around that, too. At the

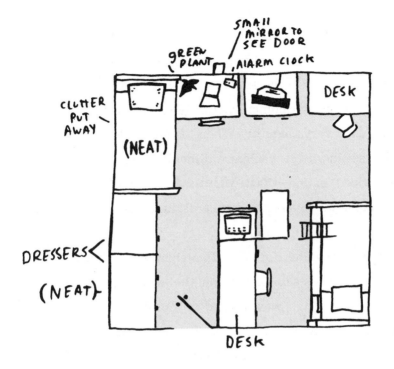

time, he had no idea what he wanted for a job, but he was clear about what he didn't want: He didn't want to work in a grocery store. He thought he'd prefer a job doing something outside. (**Note:** Money abounds in the universe. So when you focus on attracting more, get rid of the "I'm so broke" energy and begin to feel the abundance. Surround yourself with things that represent abundance and recognize abundance everywhere.)

7 Clear the wardrobe, which is located in the Knowledge area. This will help with studies.

TA-DAAAAHHHHH!

Tom was a very adept student of feng shui. He reversed his sleeping position so that he faced the door. He moved the clock away from his head and he straightened up his bookcase and desk. Within a few weeks, Tom called to say that he noticed "some very positive coincidences." When he'd cleaned his room, things went very smoothly. When his stuff piled up, procrastination set in and it was more difficult to get things done. He also noticed that he **accomplished more** when he was neat. He stopped misplacing assignments, had less trouble completing his work on time, and got better grades on tests.

An amusing anecdote that Tom shared was that right after he switched his sleeping position, the "worst kid," as he termed the guy, on his hall was "kicked out" and when his room was messy again, the kid came back. Tom made these connections. We just smiled and said, "Um-hmmmm."

And you'll never guess what else happened. Out of the blue, Tom was given a round-trip plane ticket to California so that he could visit his girlfriend there. He didn't expect a result like that! Heh.

There were some other coincidences that he noticed, but he didn't want to share them with us. He did tell us that he'd learned a lot and knew he could **get a head start** on his sophomore year by setting up his room with feng shui in mind at the outset.

9 More Gua Fixes (for under 99¢)

Did you come up with some changes for each gua on your own?
I figured you would, but here are some more just in case.

Gua	Fix
1	Cut a circle out of aluminum foil or a shiny metallic material. Write your career intentions on a small slip of paper and attach it to one side. Place this shiny side up in your Career gua or the Career area of your desk or your closet.
2	Place a great picture of you and a friend (smiling and having a good time together) in the back right-hand corner of your desk.
3	Create a small tree out of green and brown pipe cleaners. Write your intentions — about your family, your health — on small slips of paper. Roll these up very small and attach to the tree.
4	Move one of your most valuable treasures to this area. Think of all your blessings and all the abundance you have in your life whenever you see this.
5	Join seven ribbons, each one a color of the rainbow. Cut into an increment of nine inches and hang it on your doorknob. The rainbow colors can help you bring balance.
6	Gather six round stones and place them together in this area. Set your intentions around synchronicity, help from others, etc.
7	Draw the most serene and relaxing picture that you can. Place it in the left center of your room, desk, or closet.
8	Tack up an image of Athena here or create a small altar for her, because she is the Greek goddess of wisdom.
9	Draw nine goldfish and set them in the center back of your space with clear intentions about how you want to be known.

Chinese
Natal Animals

If you're in the process of choosing a roommate for next semester, or you want to better understand why you and your current roommate(s) aren't getting along so well, take a look at the Chinese natal animal charts on pages 110 and 122. In Chinese astrology, you can identify types of people you're likely to be compatible with and those with whom relationships may be a bit more, ahem, challenging.

Your Chinese natal animal is derived from the year in which you were born. In the Chinese tradition, an animal and one of the five elements represent the energy of each year. For instance, 2005 is the year of the Yin Wood Rooster and 2006 is the year of the Yang Fire Dog. Many Chinese restaurants have place mats that describe your Chinese natal animal. Just as with the daily horoscope in the newspaper, you shouldn't take this too seriously, as it represents only one part of your personality.

But who wants to be serious anyway? And if you know the animals that are in your chart (and in those of your friends and family), it will help you understand why you totally "get" some people and why you can't relate to others. Each natal animal year begins with the Chinese New Year, which runs from late January through mid-February. If you were born prior to the Chinese New Year, use the previous year for your animal sign. Or read the descriptions and see which one feels more like you! For accurate dates, refer to References and Recommended Reading (page 137) for a Chinese astrology book.

The Skinny on Each Animal

Each of the Chinese natal animals is associated with one of the five elements. If your roommate (or anyone else) is exhibiting the extreme side of his or her animal nature, you can try to balance this using the elements. After all, the five elements are the key to bringing balance through feng shui. It is also helpful to know the yin and yang quality along with the season for each animal. Yang qualities are bold and outwardly focused; yin qualities are more reserved and drawn inward.

Because there is a good chance that you and your roommate were born in the same year or an adjacent year, your animal signs will probably be compatible or at least supportive. Direct clashes occur when you are born six years apart from each other.

Determining Your Natal Animal

Your pals are those friends, family members, and colleagues with whom you are most likely to feel comfortable and at ease. You understand each other, you get along effortlessly, and you finish each other's sentences. Your opponents are those people with whom you always seem to be at odds. No matter what you do, it's never easy to be together. For animal

Birth Year: 1972, 1984, 1996

Rat
Pals: Dragon, Monkey
Opponent: Horse
Element: Yang water
Strengthen with: Metal, water
Deplete with: Wood

Birth Year: 1973, 1985, 1997

Ox
Pals: Snake, Rooster
Opponent: Sheep
Element: Yin earth
Strengthen with: Fire, earth
Deplete with: Metal

Birth Year: 1976, 1988, 2000

Dragon
Pals: Monkey, Rat
Opponent: Dog
Element: Yang water
Strengthen with: Metal, water
Deplete with: Wood

Birth Year: 1977, 1989, 2001

Snake
Pals: Rooster, Ox
Opponent: Pig
Element: Yin fire
Strengthen with: Wood, fire
Deplete with: Earth

Birth Year: 1980, 1992, 2004

Monkey
Pals: Rat, Dragon
Opponent: Tiger
Element: Yang metal
Strengthen with: Earth, metal
Deplete with: Water

Birth Year: 1981, 1993, 2005

Rooster
Pals: Ox, Snake
Opponent: Rabbit
Element: Yin metal
Strengthen with: Earth, metal
Deplete with: Water

signs not in your row, you'll find that you get along with them to vary-ing degrees. The important thing is to think about the qualities of each animal and consider how you can best complement each other. **Note:** To figure out the animal for years not listed, simply count forward or backward by 12. For instance, 1948 (a Rat year) minus 12 years is 1936; thus, 1936 is a Rat year. 2008 is also a Rat year.

Birth Year: 1974, 1986, 1998

Tiger
Pals: Horse, Dog
Opponent: Monkey
Element: Yang wood
Strengthen with: Water, wood
Deplete with: Fire

Birth Year: 1975, 1987, 1999

Rabbit
Pals: Sheep, Pig
Opponent: Rooster
Element: Yin wood
Strengthen with: Water, wood
Deplete with: Fire

Birth Year: 1978, 1990, 2002

Horse
Pals: Dog, Tiger
Opponent: Rat
Element: Yang fire
Strengthen with: Wood, fire
Deplete with: Earth

Birth Year: 1979, 1991, 2003

Sheep/Goat
Pals: Rabbit, Pig
Opponent: Ox
Element: Yin earth
Strengthen with: Fire, earth
Deplete with: Metal

Birth Year: 1982, 1994, 2006

Dog
Pals: Tiger, Horse
Opponent: Dragon
Element: Yang earth
Strengthen with: Fire, earth
Deplete with: Metal

Birth Year: 1983, 1995, 2007

Pig
Pals: Rabbit, sheep
Opponent: Snake
Element: Yin water
Strengthen with: Metal, water
Deplete with: Wood

Bear in mind, however, that relationships can be challenging when your animal elements are in opposition, such as fire and water. Clashes and opposition are not always negative, though. You know what they say: Opposites attract. What it really comes down to is balancing each other's needs.

Still not entirely clear on this? Here's the 411 on each animal:

Rat

Some famous Rats are Mandy Moore, Gwyneth Paltrow, Ben Affleck, Cameron Diaz, Eugene O'Neill, Julia Child, Jim Henson, Mikhail Baryshnikov.

People with Rat energy are very intelligent, tune in to details, and easily adapt to different circumstances. Just so you know, they are sharp little buggers who don't miss a trick. They know a good opportunity when they see one, but are quite charming. Rat people are generous and can be very romantic. Rats like to have a good time and enjoy the finer things in life. They are close to their family, very social, good at business, and great bargain hunters. On the downside, once they get an idea about something or someone, it is difficult to convince them otherwise. Unless you live for arguments, you really don't want to tangle with a Rat. If you need someone to plan a project or establish a strategy, however, go ahead and ask a Rat. He'll do a great job. Beware, though, because a Rat will use whatever information he has to his own advantage. And, uh, be careful what you tell a Rat because Rats love gossip.

Ox

Some famous Oxen are Jack Osborne, Keira Knightley, Nomar Garciaparra, Kate Beckinsale, Charlie Chaplin, Rosa Parks, B.B. King, Malcolm X.

People with Ox energy are reliable, calm, patient, dependable, and hardworking. (Did I say boring? No, of course I didn't say boring. I would never say boring.) But heads up — if you have an Ox for a roommate, don't expect wild and crazy times. Ox energy is conservative and traditional. In fact, it could be difficult to form a close relationship with an Ox. The same goes for love. Don't expect to have any one-night stands with an Ox. Ox energy is concentrated and isolated. It can also emerge as anger, frustration, and immaturity. Be careful not to cross someone with Ox energy; she'll hold a grudge like nobody's business. Ox people are not easily swayed by others, and they have to make up their own mind. So if you know an Ox, try to help her out and show her the lighter side of life. She could use it.

Tiger

Some famous Tigers are Charlotte Church, Frankie Muniz, Mary-Kate and Ashley Olsen, Agatha Christie, Groucho Marx, Ansel Adams, Jonas Salk, Bill Murray, Jay Leno.

People with Tiger energy are quick, adventurous, and optimistic. They crave excitement. They are sharp and observant, but they can also be quick-tempered. Although they are sometimes very romantic, they can also be terribly egotistical. Tigers are generally full of themselves and love nothing more than showing off. If you have a Tiger for a roommate, you may as well let him shine in the limelight and be the center of attention because when Tigers don't get everybody's attention, they get all bent out of shape. Tigers are unpredictable and often jump into situations without a lot of planning or forethought. The good news is that tigers are part cat and they always land on their feet.

Rabbit

Some famous Rabbits are Brad Pitt, Hilary Duff, BowWow, Tiger Woods, George Orwell, Orson Welles, Frank Sinatra, Billie Holiday, Marvin Gaye, John Cleese, Dale Earnhardt.

People with Rabbit energy are kind, gentle, and full of grace. They are diplomatic and sensitive but can also be very sexy. On the other hand, you don't want to tease a Rabbit too much, as Rabbits often lack confidence in themselves or have low self-esteem. And don't look for a rousing debate with a Rabbit, as he does not like conflict. More often than not, a Rabbit will tell you what you want to hear rather than what he really believes because it's the path of least resistance. Rabbits are known to be lucky. They also like to be clean. You can count on your Rabbit friends to use good judgment whenever it is needed. A word of caution: If you have a Rabbit for a roommate, try not to invade his space.

Dragon

Some famous Dragons are Courteney Cox Arquette,
Keanu Reeves, Courtney Love, Eddie Vetter, J.R.R. Tolkien,
Cole Porter, Pablo Neruda, Salvador Dalí, George Balanchine,
Maya Angelou.

Dragons are magical, fire-breathing animals. They are proud and will define themselves by what they do. Dragon people can be moody. They're not your best choice for a diplomat, because they'll express their opinions frankly, without much concern for whose feelings they might hurt. People with Dragon energy tend to do things in excess — too much shopping, too much eating, too much drinking, too much sex — you name it. One way to support your Dragon friend is to help her become aware of her tendency to indulge. But be careful: Dragons have fragile egos that bruise easily. Another way to help your Dragon friends is to encourage them to define their life purpose. Although they can accomplish wonders, they are lost without a mission. It's worth the investment in taking care of your Dragons, because they are loyal and trustworthy friends. They also tend to be quite lucky.

Snake

Some famous Snakes are Sarah Jessica Parker, Robert Downey Jr.,
Elizabeth Hurley, Moby, Pablo Picasso, Dorothy Parker, Jean-Paul Sartre,
Indira Gandhi, John F. Kennedy, Martin Luther King Jr., Bob Dylan.

People with Snake energy are wise, intuitive, and watchful, and they have an ability to read situations and identify

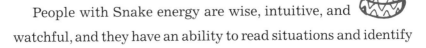

people's motives. They like calm, quiet, and the finer things in life. But watch out, because they have a need to be *right* and they need to have the *last word*. Snakes are drawn to intrigue, but they also worry a lot. Although they can be demanding, hissing, and sometimes biting, deep down they have a fear of being rejected. Snake energy is strong and powerful. It can also be venomous. In a difficult situation, you can count on Snakes to be strong. Don't cross a Snake if you don't have to — a Snake is not known for forgivenISSsssss.

Horse

Some famous Horses are Cynthia Nixon, Josh Hartnett, Aaliyah, David Schwimmer, Martha Graham, e.e. cummings, Dmitrii Shostakovich, Ella Fitzgerald, Billy Graham, Nelson Mandela, Neil Armstrong, Muhammad Ali, Stephen Hawking, Oprah Winfrey.

Horses are go, go, go and need constant stimulation. In fact, they can be rather impatient. Because they have sharp minds, they are usually popular and witty. Horses love to join other groups, so they're likely to be involved with Greek life or campus clubs. Although they like the sound of their own voice, they're not always interested in other opinions and can be a bit narrow-minded. They have big hearts and their feelings are easily hurt. When this happens, they sulk. But not to worry. Although Horses get angry easily, they don't hold a grudge.

Rather, people with Horse energy are generous and giving. One thing to remember: Horse energy is free-spirited, so people with Horse energy may also be nonconformists. They seek independence and prefer doing things according to their own schedule.

 ## Sheep/Goat

Some famous Sheep are Kurt Cobain, Faith Hill, LL Cool J, Gavin Rossdale, Babe Ruth, Katharine Hepburn, Bishop Desmond Tutu, Barbara Walters, Mikhail Gorbachev, Bill Gates, Yo-Yo Ma.

People with Sheep energy tend to be followers. They are peacemakers who seek balance and beauty. Because of their heightened sensitivity, they are known to have creative and artistic flair. In general, Sheep are good-natured and romantic. They mean well and will share what they have. They are patient and have the ability to wait out a situation. They are not great with money, however, so don't put a Sheep in charge of the finances. And while I'm mentioning their downside, Sheep are not the best decision makers. Having said that, you'll never find a better listener than a Sheep. He will listen to your tales of woe and offer lots of sympathy and compassion. So if you need a good ear to hear your side of the story, tell it to a Sheep. *Baaaaaah.*

Monkey

Some Famous Monkeys are Sarah McLachlan, Halle Berry, Christina Ricci, Ben Savage, F. Scott Fitzgerald, Ira Gershwin, Ian Fleming, Charlie Parker, Johnny Cash, Martina Navratilova.

People with Monkey energy are active, playful, clever, intelligent, and charming. A Monkey will face challenges head on and likes to take control of any situation. However, sometimes Monkeys need to loosen the reins and let go. It is a challenge for them to behave freely. Monkeys are skilled at maneuvering through difficulties and can be wonderful motivators. They can meet just about any challenge. But Monkeys have a dark side. Because they are control freaks, they usually trust only a few very close friends. By the way, don't even try to get a Monkey to talk about a touchy subject — she just won't do it. Still, Monkeys are very likable. They just need to learn how to let things flow.

Rooster

Some famous Roosters are Britney Spears, Elijah Wood, Justin Timberlake, Jennifer Aniston, Simon Wiesenthal, Eudora Welty, Susan Sontag, Diane Sawyer, Itzhak Perlman, Debbie Harry.

Roosters have an active, nervous, and somewhat anxious energy (they're worriers). They will weigh both sides of an issue and fret over the negatives. As a result, they tend to procrastinate, unable to make a decision. They are good providers, like to talk, and are perfectionists. They also LURVE attention. Roosters have the ability to accomplish a lot, but they may get sidetracked by their fears. Here's a typical Rooster scenario: She wants a relationship, yet fears it at the same time. Thus, nothing happens except a lot of fret and worry. Although Roosters often have big egos, they are tireless workers. So try not to criticize a Rooster. Although she may steamroll over someone if she wants something done, she can't handle criticism (that big ol' ego of hers makes her sensitive).

Dog

Some famous Dogs are Kirsten Dunst, Prince William, Uma Thurman, Chris O'Donnell, Al Capone, George Gershwin, René Magritte, Mother Teresa, Jane Goodall, Gloria Steinem.

People with Dog energy are lovable, honest, intelligent, and dependable. However, like the Rooster, they tend to worry about things unnecessarily. Dogs put family and home first. Thus, if your roommate is a Dog, his room will be very important to him, like a wolf's den. Be careful about letting anyone enter the Dog's space or touch his things without permission (unless you want to get bit. *Woof!*). Dogs are very territorial. In addition, Dogs have high standards and morals. Don't be surprised if your Dog friend sits in judgment on your lifestyle. He doesn't mean you harm; it's just his way. People with Dog energy make loyal and lovable companions. After all, the Dog is man's best friend. Whatever you do, the Dog will always be happy to see you and will always greet you (we hope he won't *slobber* all over you, but you never know). The Dog may also hide out in his room (or den, as he likes to think of it), as he is easily frightened. Your Dog friends may need help building relationships: These are scary to them, particularly intimate relationships. Dogs take a long time to get with a love interest.

Pig

Some famous Pig people are Ewan McGregor, Tupac Shakur, Jada Pinkett Smith, Ricky Martin, Vladimir Nabokov, Duke Ellington, Ronald Reagan, Henry Kissinger, Elvis Presley, His Holiness the Dalai Lama, Woody Allen, David Letterman.

People with Pig energy love to indulge in pleasure. They are honest, and can be very nice, generous, gregarious, and passionate. They work hard, yet they may have little self-control. Because Pigs are so generous, they may think it is okay to help themselves or borrow from others without asking permission (uh, whoops, not stealing exactly, just borrowing). People with Pig energy have a tendency to overpromise and under-deliver, although you can count on a Pig friend to bail you out of trouble. Pigs are lucky and determined, but they sometimes lack self-confidence and feel that they are not beautiful. Pigs need to realize that beauty comes from the inside out. They will go to great lengths to avoid humiliation and ridicule. Watch out for depression and self-destructive tendencies in your Pig friends. At times, Pig energy can also be slow and sluggish. The Pig needs to know and trust that things will work out just fine.

Animals and Stars

Even though you were born in the year of a particular animal, chances are that you have other animals and animal energy in your astrological chart. To gain a deeper insight into yourself, your family, your professors, and your friends, note the following correspondence between the natal animal and Western astrological signs.

Chinese Animal	Western Sign	Chinese Animal	Western Sign
Rat	Aries	Horse	Libra
Ox	Taurus	Sheep/Goat	Scorpio
Tiger	Gemini	Monkey	Sagittarius
Rabbit	Cancer	Rooster	Capricorn
Dragon	Leo	Dog	Aquarius
Snake	Virgo	Pig	Pisces

A Field Guide to Natal Animals

Here's a synopsis of animal energies to keep in mind for key situations.

	As a Roommate	In Class	At a Party
Rat	Will find great bargains. May also keep clutter around.	May do whatever is necessary to further himself.	Will be very social.
Ox	Will be patient and put up with many things. Look out if you get on her angry side.	Will establish regular study habits and stick to them. Very dependable.	Will organize the party. If you need some rules, let the Ox handle them.
Tiger	Will bring spontaneity and excitement to the room and dorm.	Will plunge right in without a plan and still end up successful.	Will be unpredictable.
Rabbit	Will try not to hurt your feelings and will tell you what you want to hear.	May find a nice, quiet spot in the library, away from others.	Will have a nice time, away from the spotlight.
Dragon	Will be loyal and trustworthy. May also carve out new paths and explode occasionally.	Will dive in and get the job done, although sometimes in an unconventional way.	Will enjoy the excitement and will motivate others to have a party.
Snake	Will keep her own counsel and will make sure she has some of the finer things in life. Likes privacy.	Will depend on herself (rather than others) and will actively pursue her goals.	Will create mystery and go to the finest parties.

	As a Roommate	In Class	At a Party
Horse	May listen to you, but won't be genuinely interested in your opinion.	Will make his own hours and work at his own pace until the job is done.	Will wear himself out!
Sheep/ Goat	Will go to great lengths to accommodate you. You can count on her to do the right thing.	Will worry that she won't get everything done. Once she makes a decision, however, she'll stay focused.	Will blow the budget, add a romantic flair, and also keep the peace.
Monkey	Will solve the difficult situation, but show little sympathy.	Can memorize whatever is necessary to get through the test.	Will be popular and full of life.
Rooster	Will respond positively to flattery. Will tell you exactly what she thinks.	Might be distracted and check everyone out in the library. In the end, she will focus and pull through.	Will be the center of attention.
Dog	You can always depend on this roommate to be fair.	Will help good friends pull through when in a jam.	Will relax and spend time with friends.
Pig	You can count on him to be honest. Will expect you to share, just as he does.	Loves the social part of studying! Probably won't get his work done early.	Will have a great time. May overdo things.

The Elements
& Personalities

Everyone's personality has elemental qualities. These are the qualities of water, wood, fire, earth, and metal. Don't start thinking that one is better than another. It's not. Each quality stands on its own and simply is. So if you are living with a roommate who seems to be Merry Sunshine one day and Godzilla the next, step back and take a look at the qualities of her emotions. To the right is a chart to help you make adjustments in your space to balance the energy.

Perhaps you are the roommate with the mood swings. If you are feeling like there is too much of one emotion, make an adjustment to minimize or reduce the element that causes it. Conversely, if you'd like to see more of a particular emotion, add the element that creates or supports it.

For example, when you feel apathetic, bring in a green plant to help bring the attributes of the wood element into balance. For those days when you want to yell at everyone, minimize the color green, stripe patterns, flowers, and plants. Another way to balance excess wood is to add some red or hang pictures of people or animals.

	In Balance	Too Much	Too Little
Wood	Confident	Angry, hostile, irresponsible	Apathetic, irritable
Fire	Motivated	Can't get enough, fears separation	Cold, dull, shy
Earth	Nurturing	Smothering, overprotective, worries constantly	Lacks stability, emotionally closed
Metal	Thinks clearly	Critical, sarcastic	Sloppy, has difficulty focusing
Water	Clever, curious	Detached, lonely	Fearful, stingy

The Energy of Color

Colors have the ability to lift us up and drag us down, so it is important to use colors that you truly love. Chances are, you are not allowed to paint your walls. (Let's hope they aren't anti-freeze green or reform school gray.) However, you can bring in color through curtains, bedspreads, posters, and whatever else your imagination can think up. Is that your white refrigerator? Then what's to stop you from covering it in wallpaper or paint or sticker art?

How you use color is important. When you introduce color with intention and align it with its appropriate qualities, you have some serious power in your hands. To the right is a summary of the energy generated by common colors. You may have already intuited some of these energies, but others may surprise you. Take a good look at the wheel — you won't be getting a pop quiz or anything, but it will be helpful to know this stuff later on.

Don't be limited to the colors in your room. Color is part of your daily life. There are all kinds of ways to shift your energies through the use of color: in the clothes you wear, the foods you eat, the people you surround yourself with. For example, if you'd like to be fired up one day, wear some red. If it's your health you want to boost, wear some green. If you'd like to cool off a bit, put on something that is black or dark blue. White will help you be alert and cut right through a problem. Yellow helps strengthen communication and brings focus.

Try it for yourself and see what you can make happen.

The Wheel of Color

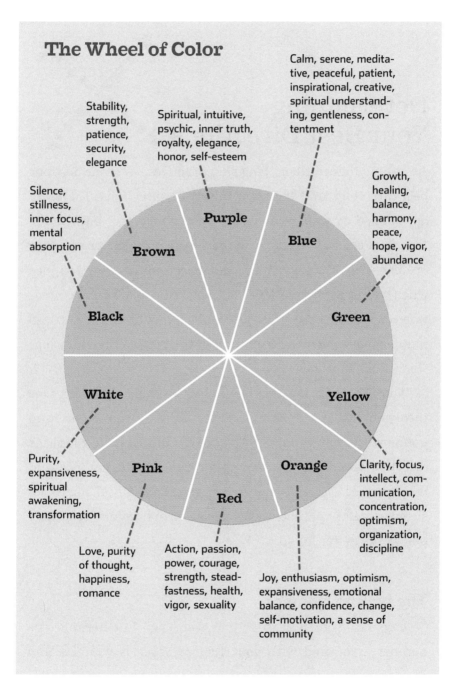

Calm, serene, meditative, peaceful, patient, inspirational, creative, spiritual understanding, gentleness, contentment

Stability, strength, patience, security, elegance

Spiritual, intuitive, psychic, inner truth, royalty, elegance, honor, self-esteem

Silence, stillness, inner focus, mental absorption

Purple

Blue

Growth, healing, balance, harmony, peace, hope, vigor, abundance

Brown

Black

Green

White

Yellow

Purity, expansiveness, spiritual awakening, transformation

Pink

Orange

Clarity, focus, intellect, communication, concentration, optimism, organization, discipline

Red

Love, purity of thought, happiness, romance

Action, passion, power, courage, strength, steadfastness, health, vigor, sexuality

Joy, enthusiasm, optimism, expansiveness, emotional balance, confidence, change, self-motivation, a sense of community

Determining
Your Best Directions

According to traditional feng shui practices, everyone has four best directions and four less favorable directions. These are determined by your personal Trigram, which goes back to the *I Ching*. Personal Trigrams are based on your gender and year of birth. The directions are *facing* directions . . . how you face when you sit at your desk or at a table. To find out which direction you should set up your desk and bed, for instance, you need to know your personal Trigram. I have given you the information you need below.

Note: There are two theories on best sleeping directions. One theory holds that it is the direction to which the top of your head points when you lie in bed. The second theory is that it is the direction you face, when facing forward: where you look and what you see. Don't be confused by this. Basically, if you're not sleeping well, experiment with these two options and see which one works better for you.

The Lo Shu Number

To calculate your best directions, you need to determine the number associated with your Trigram. This is your Lo Shu number, which is simply another feng shui term. The calculation is different for males vs. females.

Women use the following formula:

1 Add all the digits in your birth year.

2 Reduce to a single digit (add the first number to the second).

3 Add 4 (reduce to a single digit again if you need to).

For example, a female born in 1985: **1 + 9 + 8 + 5 = 23**. Add the first number and the second to get a single digit: **2 + 3 = 5**. Add 4 to that digit: **5 + 4 = 9**. The result is your Lo Shu number.

If you are a male, to determine your Lo Shu number, you:

1 Add the digits in your birth year.

2 Reduce to a single digit (add the first number to the second).

3 Subtract the number you got in step 2 from 11.

For example, a male born in 1985: **1 + 9 + 8 + 5 = 23**. Add the first number and the second to get a single digit: **2 + 3 = 5**. Subtract that digit from 11: **11 − 5 = 6**.

Thus, for people born in 1985, the Lo Shu number for women is 9 and for men is 6.

Note: If you are born in January through February 4, use the year before as your birth year. Also, if you ended up with 5, change to 8 if you are female and 2 if you are male.

Once you know your Lo Shu number, determine which directional group you are in: East or West.

1, 3, 4, and 9 are related to the East group Trigrams.

2, 6, 7, and 8 are related to the West group Trigrams.

There is no Trigram for the number 5. That's why if you end up with 5, you switch it to 8 if you are female and 2 if you are male.

The best directions for the East group are north, south, east, and southeast.

East Group

TRIGRAMS & LO SHU NUMBERS				
	Water #1	Thunder #3	Wind #4	Fire #9
L1*	SE	S	N	E
L2	S	SE	E	N
L3	E	N	S	SE
L4	N	E	SE	S
U1	W	SW	NW	NE
U2	NW	NE	W	SW
U3	NE	NW	SW	W
U4	SW	W	NE	NW

* See the chart at the top of page 132 for a description of each category.

L = lucky or auspicious   U = unlucky or inauspicious

The best directions for the West Group are west, northeast, northwest, and southwest.

The remaining directions are your unfavorable directions. Observe how you feel when you face one of your favorable directions as compared to one of your unfavorable directions.

Use the following chart to determine the best directions by Trigram. Refer to the chart at the top of page 132 for the meaning of each category.

West Group

TRIGRAMS & LO SHU NUMBERS			
Earth #2	Heaven #6	Lake #7	Mountain #8
L1*	NE	W	NW	SW
L2	NW	SW	NE	W
L3	W	NE	SW	NW
L4	SW	NW	W	NE
U1	E	SE	N	S
U2	S	N	SE	E
U3	SE	E	S	N
U4	N	S	E	SE

* See the chart at the top of page 132 for a description of each category.

L = lucky or auspicious   U = unlucky or inauspicious

Most & Least Favorable Facing Directions

Direction	Result
L1	Best overall facing, prosperity, respectability; great location for bedroom, study, front door
L2	Longevity, romantic relationships; excellent cure-all position for family problems
L3	Good health, harmonious relationships
L4	Best sleep, peace, stability, general good fortune
U1	Least unlucky position; accidents, arguments, injury
U2	Failed relationships, missed opportunities, malicious encounters
U3	Accidents, injury, fire, loss of employment, litigation
U4	Unproductive careers, disease, general misfortune

Directions, Lo Shu Numbers, Trigrams & Elements

Direction	Lo Shu #	Trigram	Element
North	1	Water	Water
Northeast	8	Mountain	Earth
East	3	Thunder	Wood
Southeast	4	Wind	Wood
South	9	Fire	Fire
Southwest	2	Earth	Earth
West	7	Lake	Metal
Northwest	6	Heaven	Metal

As you know by now, the answer in feng shui is always in the elements. When the elements are in balance, there is balance and an easy flow to your life. If you'd like to learn more about the five elements, an excellent resource is *Between Heaven and Earth* (see the References and Recommended Reading section at the end of the book).

Reinforcing Your Changes

What the heck? Secret powers? Do you need a Spider-Man decoder ring? A Power Rangers Raptor Cycle? A couple of *Star Wars* light sabers? No, no, NO (not that those aren't pretty cool).

How to Use the Three Secrets Reinforcement

Let me explain. The Three Secrets Reinforcement is a sacred practice used in Black Sect Feng Shui as a means of strengthening and empowering any cure you want to implement utilizing your body, speech, and mind. (Translation: This puts the big whammy in your mojo.)

Before I go any further, there's something I want to say. *Sshhhhhhhhh.* As in, tighten loose lips. When you make changes from a feng shui perspective, keep the changes to yourself. Resist the temptation to tell all your friends. Obviously, if you're doing changes or adjustments with your roomie, you're gonna have to talk about it. However, if you are doing them on your own, keep them to yourself. When you tell people about them, you dilute the energy, the effect, and the outcome. Remember, everything is energy. Keeping your energy concentrated and focused makes a huge difference in the outcome.

Okay, now that I've got that out of the way, here's what I want to tell you. The power of your personal intention is what gives the Three Secrets their energy. Moving a bed or desk, hanging a mirror or crystal — c'mon, just doing that is not a big deal, right? What makes it a big deal is how you *think* about what you're doing.

To apply intention, you must be clear about what you want. Now, that sounds easy, but try it. Not so easy, is it? Did about 38 different ideas and wants just scramble across your brain waves? Don't stress — it happens to all of us. Try it again. Get very specific. Get very focused. What is it that you want most? Let the rest fall away for right now. You can always come back to other desires once you've taken care of this first one.

Now that you have the specific goal in mind, there are three steps you must take:

1 You need to visualize your goal. To do this best, vividly imagine that what you want is real and feel what it would be like to have this goal come true. Then simply add two more steps.

2 Use a *mudra* (a spiritual hand gesture) to align your body with the desired energetic outcome. In Black Sect Feng Shui, the ousting or expelling mudra is commonly used. Hold down the middle and ring fingers with your thumb. Your first finger and little finger will be straight up. Flick out the middle and ring fingers in a snapping motion. This action removes obstacles from your life, thus allowing blessings to come in. FYI: Women use their right hand and men use their left hand in this mudra. You may use any personal spiritual hand gesture from your tradition or any other one that is comfortable for you.

3 Use sacred words, prayers, or sounds to bless and strengthen cures. If you don't know any, here's one, the mantra of compassion, that works well: Om Ma Ni Pad Me Hum (pronounced ohm-mah-nee-pahd-mee-hum). Reciting this or any other mantra or prayer of your choosing is a way to connect you with the divine.

Let's review. See it. Flick it. Bless it. Oh, and make sure to do this *nine* times.

Once you've named it, and seen it, and felt it, hold this vision in your mind and know that it's coming true for you. Do this at any and all small moments in your day. When you're outside a classroom waiting to go in. When you're standing in line at the dining hall. At night, just before you fall asleep. In the morning, when you're lying in bed and thinking of the day ahead.

As if that's not enough to keep you busy, here are a couple of things for you to think about.

The most powerful time to make your changes is between 11:00 in the morning and 1:00 in the afternoon. These two hours are the most active, yang part of each day. The sun is highest in the sky during these periods.

You can also use moon cycles to help you with your changes. If you are looking to attract things to yourself or to bring in new energy (such as better study habits, money, synchronicity), try doing your changes in the period between the new moon and the full moon. This is a two-week period of rising energy and growth. It's an energetic cycle. If you are letting go of things (bad habits, clutter, unproductive relationships), do your changes after the full moon and before the new moon. The full moon is the height of energy. The time after the full moon is a period of letting go. It's a great time to clean out and start fresh.

Remember, thought creates reality. What you spend your time thinking about is what you will bring to yourself. So don't keep saying things like, "I'm such a loser," and "I'm so fat," and "I'm always broke." If you do, it reinforces your situation. Here's a better way to set intentions. Repeat the following phrases: "I'm loved"; "I love my body"; "I have more than enough."

Oh, one more thing. Never, never, never use feng shui for negative reasons or to do harm to anyone or anything. What you put out into the world comes back to you. If you send out mean-spirited thoughts, they will return to YOU. Focus on yourself. Let other people's lives unfold as they're supposed to (even if what they're doing makes no sense to you). Keep seeing the positive and that is what the universe will reflect back to you.

References & Recommended Reading

For Feng Shui

Chinese Power Animals, Pamela Leigh Powers. Boston: Samuel Weiser, Inc., 2000.

Clear Your Clutter with Feng Shui, Karen Kingston. New York: Broadway Books, 2000.

The Complete Idiot's Guide to Feng Shui, Elizabeth Moran, Master Joseph Yu, and Master Val Biktashev. New York: Penguin, Alpha Books, 2002.

The Complete Illustrated Guide to Feng Shui, Lillian Too. London: Element Books Limited, 1996.

Creating Sacred Space with Feng Shui, Karen Kingston. New York: Broadway Books, 1997.

Feng Shui Astrology, Jon Sandifer. New York: Ballantine Books, 1997.

Feng Shui Dos and Taboos, Angi Ma Wong. North Adams, MA: Storey Publishing, 2000.

Feng Shui for the Soul, Denise Linn. Carlsbad, CA: Hay House, Inc, 1999.

Feng Shui Handbook, Master Lam Kam Chuen. New York: Owl Books, 1996.

Feng Shui: Harmony by Design, Nancy Santopietro. New York: Penguin, Perigee Books, 1996.

Feng Shui and Health, Nancy Santopietro. New York: Three Rivers Press, 2002.

Feng Shui Made Easy, William Spear. San Francisco: Harper San Franscisco, 1995.

Feng Shui, The Chinese Art of Placement, Sarah Rossbach. London: Penguin, Arcana, 1983, 2000.

Interior Design with Feng Shui, Sarah Rossbach. London: Penguin, Arcana, 1991, 2000.

The Modern Book of Feng Shui, Steven Post. New York: Dell Publishing, 1998.

Move Your Stuff, Change Your Life, Karen Rauch Carter. New York: Fireside, 2000.

The Practical Encyclopedia of Feng Shui, Gill Hale. London: Lorenz Books, 2002.

Sacred Space, Denise Linn. New York: Ballantine Wellspring, 1995.

The Western Guide to Feng Shui, Terah Kathryn Collins. Carlsbad, CA: Hay House, 1996.

The Western Guide to Feng Shui Room by Room, Terah Kathryn Collins. Carlsbad, CA: Hay House, 1999.

For I Ching

A Guide to the I Ching, Carol K. Anthony. Stow, MA: Anthony Publishing Company, 1988.

The I Ching or Book of Changes, Brian Brown Walker. New York: St. Martin's Griffin, 1992.

I Ching: The Book of Changes and the Unchanging Truth, Hua-Ching Ni. Los Angeles: Seven Star Communications, 1983, 1990, 1994.

The Illustrated I Ching, R. L. Wing. New York: Doubleday, 1982.

The Philosophy of the I Ching, Carol K. Anthony. Stow, MA: Anthony Publishing Company, 1998.

For Self-Improvement, Intuition, Law of Attraction, and Setting Intention

Ask and It Is Given: Learning to Manifest Your Desires, Ester and Jerry Hicks. Hay House, 2004.

Awakening Intuition, Mona Lisa Schulz, M.D., Ph.D. New York: Three Rivers Press, 1998.

Between Heaven and Earth: A Guide to Chinese Medicine, Harriet Beinfield, L.Ac, and Efram Korngold, L.Ac., O.M.D. New York: Ballantine Wellspring, 1991.

Conversations with God, Book 1, Neale Donald Walsch. G.P. Putnam's Sons, 1996.

Conversations with God, Book 2, Neale Donald Walsch. Charlottesville, VA: Hampton Roads, 1997.

Conversations with God, Book 3, Neale Donald Walsch. Charlottesville, VA: Hampton Roads, 1998.

Dowsing for Health, Dr. Patrick Mac-Manaway. London: Lorenz Books, 2001.

Excuse Me, Your Life Is Waiting, Lynn Grabhorn. Charlottesville, VA: Hampton Roads, 2000.

Manifest Your Destiny, Wayne W. Dyer. London: HarperPerennial, 1997.

The Power of Intention: Learning to Co-Create Your World Your Way, Wayne W. Dyer. Carlsbad, CA: Hay House, 2004.

The Power of Now, Eckhart Tolle. Novato, CA: New World Library, 1999.

Power vs. Force: The Hidden Determinants of Human Behavior, David R. Hawkins, M.D., Ph.D. Carlsbad, CA: Hay House, 1995, 1998, 2002.

Soul Coaching: 28 Days to Discover Your Authentic Self, Denise Lynn. Carlsbad, CA: Hay House, 2003.

You Can Heal Your Life, Louise Hay. Carlsbad, CA: Hay House, 1984, 1987.

Other

How to Grow Fresh Air, Dr. B. C. Wolverton. New York: Penguin, 1996.

Web Resources

www.clearhomeclearheart.com
Eric Dowsett's Web site

www.fengshuiconnections.com
Feng Shui Connections

www.fengshuidirectory.com
Feng Shui Directory

www.internationalfengshuiguild.org
International Feng Shui Guild

www.lessemf.com
Less EMF News

www.luckycat.com
Feng Shui Emporium

www.neschoolfengshui.com
New England School of Feng Shui

www.wsfs.com
Western School of Feng Shui

www.yunlintemple.org
Yun Lin Temple

Index

Note: References in **bold** refer to charts and diagrams.

F

fame (gua 9), **21**, 56–59
  health/body connection, 59
  solutions for, 58–59
  what's in and out, **59**
family gua (gua 3), **20**, 31–34
  health/body connection, 34
  solutions to, 33–34
  what's in and out, **34**
feng shui
  Black Sect, 133, 134
  job-finding help, 26
  positive focus of, 136
five elements, 8–9, 109

G

gender, 128–129
goals, 22–23, 134
gua fixes, **17, 60, 101, 107**. *See also*
  specific gua(s)

H

health/body connection, 77. *See also*
  under specific gua(s)
helpful people and travel (gua 6), **21**,
  44–47
  health/body connection, 47
  solutions to, 46–47
  what's in and out, **47**

I

I Ching, **21–22**, 128
intention, 15, 76, 79–80, 85, 126, 134

J

jobs and internships, 26, 37

K

knowledge (gua 8), **20**, 52–55
  health/body connection, 54–55
  solutions for, 54
  what's in and out, **55**

L

Lo Shu number, 128–129, 132

M

meditation, 41, 51, 87
mnemonic, 80
mom, 27, 30
mudra, 134–135

P

pairs, 28, 29
personalities, 15, 124–127
philanthropy, 36, 37
plants, 69, 95
problem situations
  bookshelves, 75
  closets, 72–73
  dressers and bureaus, 74
  knickknacks and tchotchkes, 75, 88
  messy roommates, 75–76
  pictures and posters, 71–72
  storage bins, 73–74
  trash can, 71, 83, 92–93
  under your bed, 74–75
  See also EMFs
procrastination, 93–95, 106
prosperity gua (gua 4), **20**, 35–39
  health/body connection, 39
  solutions to, 38–39
  what's in and out, **39**

Q

questionnaire, 18–19, 51

R

recycling, 89
relationship gua (gua 2), **21**, 27–30
  health/body connection, 30
  solutions to, 29–30
  what's in and out, **30**
roommates, 16. *See also under*
  dorm room

S

seasons, 23, 32, 51
sleep, 64–67, 91–93, 99–100
spiritual hand gesture, 134–135
sun and moon, 58, 59, 135–136
synchronicity, 44, 136

T

three C's, 80
Three Secrets Reinforcement, 87,
  133–136
Trigram, **21–22**, 128–131, **132**

Y

yin and yang, **11**, 109